伙 伴 行

Leonoir and Gingerlet
(also starring a gaggle of sidekicks)

著述：季 晨
Narrator: Chen JI

插画：蒋 端
Illustrator: Duan JIANG

南京大学出版社

目录　Table of Contents

自我介绍 / Who We Are	1
开场白 / By Way of Introduction	3
缘起 / Where the Idea Came From	7
我的根 / Familial Context	9
遥远的记忆 / Earliest Memory	13
出气筒小黄 / Gingerlet, the Pushover	16
蒙特维多的邂逅（外一则）/ A Stalker in Montevideo (with a bonus picture)	20
黑狮粉墨登场 / Enter Leonoir	24
重逢，情难抑 / The Unbearable Happiness of Reuniting	28
大胃王小猫 / The Kitten That Eats Like a Pig	34
自给自足的黄渔翁 / The Self-Sufficient Fishercat	38
智力测验 / IQ Test	42
护鱼卫士 / The Catcher Watcher	44
拦路抢劫 / The Catch Snatcher	49
茅房纪实 / Legend of Thatched Cottages	54
偶遇 / An Encounter of Destiny	59
收获 / The Harvest	65
偶像小鹤 / My Childhood Best Friend	67
香椿的口福 / A Boon to the Toon	74
智胜 / A Battle of Wits	77
有肉不欢 / One Man's Meat Is Leonoir's Poison	81
藏宝记 / If You Can't Eat It, Bury It	86
罗汉斋 / A Monk's Diet	90
"攀"比 / Getting a Cat's Eye View	94
地盘争夺战 / Turf War	97

侠客传奇 / Dr Peace Lover and Mr Rat Hunter	…………	101
义气 / The Sanctity of Friendship	…………	106
弹弓枪 / Catapult Pistols	…………	109
弹弓 / The Hand Catapult	…………	118
大鸟的故事 / The Big Bird	…………	124
郭逗和插刀 / The Sisters	…………	129
鸡拳秘笈 / Hen-Style Kungfu	…………	134
双姝戏蛇 / The Duel	…………	137
矢记 / Foul Play	…………	139
小黄出走 / Goodbye, Gingerlet	…………	142
黑狮迷踪 / Adieu, Leonoir	…………	144
蓦然回首 / Was It Real or Was It a Dream?	…………	147
写在最后 / Last But Not Least	…………	150

Leonoir and Gingerlet　伙伴行

自我介绍　Who We Are

我叫季晨，以翻译为生，成天在中英文之间来回倒腾。以前是自由职业，口笔译兼顾，现在是全职口译。多年前曾在母校南京大学教英文，闲来也编编词典。My name is JI Chen. I make a living from language conversion, between Chinese and English. I used to be amphibious, active in both translation and interpretation, but am now a full-time conference interpreter. Once upon a time, I worked in my alma mater, Nanjing University, as an English teacher and as a lexicographer of sorts.

这是我和儿子在颐和园的自拍。This is a selfie of me and my son, in the Summer Palace of Beijing. Or should we call it Winter Palace in this case?

父子，颐和园。*Father and son, in Summer Palace, Beijing.*

季麦天,于南戴河。*Tian Macleod Ji, in Nandaihe.*

　　说起我儿子,他是此书的第一读者。他叫季麦天,母语是英语,主修汉语和电影制作,学习之余,兼职平面模特,赚些零花钱。*Speaking of my son, this book was originally meant for him and for him only. Tian Macleod JI (yes, a fusion name he has) is a native English speaker studying Chinese as well as filmmaking. He also does modelling on the side, to help support his studies.*

　　感谢丁宁,在本书创作、定稿过程中提出极为宝贵的修改意见,态度严肃认真、不留情面,后期审校亦尽心尽责,她的贡献无声地流淌在本书的字里行间。*My unqualified gratitude goes to Ning DING for her valuable and invaluable contributions in her capacity as a highly critical critique partner and a highly professional proofreader. Without this acknowledgement, she would have been an unsung heroine, whose input flows silently throughout the book.*

丁宁,在家。*Ning DING, at home.*

Leonoir and Gingerlet　伙伴行

开场白　By Way of Introduction

　　上文提到，此书原本只是写给儿子的（忆旧笔记兼汉语泛读），后来打算出版。因此我得想想：还有哪些朋友可能会想读、爱读，并从中获益？Initially, this book was intended as a 'familial memory'. Its secondary function, as an instructive reader for my son, was an afterthought. Now that I've decided to have it published for wider circulation, a question has come up: Who else would be reading it, and could potentially benefit from it? 三思后发觉目标读者群难以框定，亦似无需框定，大致包括学英语学翻译的中国人，也不排除母语为英语、正在学汉语的老外，从事翻译工作或有志于翻译事业的，或许也可以从中找到一些灵感和启发。当然，若有志同道合爱猫爱狗、兼爱飞禽走兽之人，茶余饭后捧读此书觉得有消遣之效，那也算是歪打正着。To set a range of rigid parameters with which to define the book's target readership would be challenging, and perhaps unnecessary. Chinese readers who are studying English may find it 'useful'. The same goes for foreign students of the Chinese language whose default medium of thinking is English. You are a translator or interpreter? Or training to be one? It may turn a few lights on for you so you can access some overlooked angles. Others may pick it up for leisure reading if the topics appeal to them and/or they find it entertaining to compare notes with another pet owner, although I'd be very surprised, and rather upset, if this book ended up on the pets and vets shelf.

　　虽说是双语创作，中英文却并非亦步亦趋、机械对应。两种文本就像记忆的钟声，激荡在相向的回音壁上，它们是呼应关系，相辅相成，却不一定如出一辙。This is a bilingual book, but it's not one in which Chinese and English texts track each other in lockstep in perfect symmetry. The parallel texts are resonant chimes from the bell toll of my memory bouncing off opposite walls: They do not so much *mirror* and *mimic* as *echo* and *complement* each other. 说实话，权威翻译教科书汗牛充栋，我凭疏才浅学，试图挤进人才济济的学术殿堂，无异于以一粟投沧海、以一苇渡浩波。Let's face it: There is already a plethora of how-to's - instructive works of authoritative standing - in this profession. I am honoured to bask in reflected glory through my association with some of their authors, but I would not hesitate to call myself an impostor if I presumed to be part of that glory, for I am neither equipped nor ready to do so. 故而本书绝非汉译英实例汇编，其标新立异之处，恰恰在于笔者创作时，不是先用某一种语言构思、笔录，再转译成另一种语言，而是用两种语言分别独立构思、独立笔录，相向而行，所谓"一事两说"也。It is therefore not my intention for this to be a conventional textbook, to show how I translate between two languages, which would entail mentally formulating the story in either of the two languages first, writing it down in that language and subsequently converting the writing to the other language. Rather, this book differentiates itself by attempting to tell *one* story in *two* languages, with the author putting on the Chinese hat and the English hat alternately. Yes, a bilingual storyteller - that's me. 这样既可以避免程式化翻译的僵硬，还能潜移默化，帮助学生养成用外语思考的习惯，摆脱母语的干扰，达事半功倍之效。笔者希望借助此书，读者能更加自如地适用两种语言中的任何一种去思考并表达，不再需要先用母语思考，然后在脑海中翻译成英语再说出来。This format, I believe, lends itself to greater fluidity, so it reads better in both languages. An added bonus that comes with this style is its potential to help students develop the habit of thinking *directly* in their non-native language, independently of their mother tongue. Hopefully, reading this book can help ease you into this dual-track mode where you can formulate what you wish to say in the language that you are going to say it in, obviating the need for mental translation. 为此，笔者思绪行云流水，中英文意群交替，随想随录，一气呵成，事后不作次序调整，以保留口述轶事之流畅感。不过，为了避免版面过于凌乱，一律中文先行，英文随

后,尽管最先闯进脑海的语言可能是英文,不一定是中文。To that end, you will be reading the passages in the same order as I wrote them: one or more sentences in Chinese followed by one or more in English. This order, where Chinese sits in front of English on the tandem bike, so to speak, is in the interest of readability, but the language in which a thought was first formulated could have been either of them. To maintain the flow of the narrative that characterises verbal storytelling, continuity of thought was prioritised and faithfully reproduced, with no *post hoc* re-ordering whatsoever. 当然,所谓"独立"表述,也不是绝对的,如果回忆的画面在脑海里先以汉语化为文字,那么下一个瞬间的英语复述,难免不受到汉语的影响,如"影"随"形",反之亦然,因此翻译成分不可谓无。Be that as it may, that each story is related in two languages *separately* does not preclude an element of *translation* in its conventional sense, owing to sequentiality: The first language, be it Chinese or English, in which a certain graphical memory is converted into a lexical representation in my head is comparable to a boat that sets sail first; the other language, in which the same story is *retold* in the next instant, is another boat trailing along in the first boat's wake.

既然笔者的初衷是写一本话题轻松的轶事集,不是严格意义上的教科书,那么在遣词造句方面,也就没有刻意雕琢出教科书的范儿。Since this is more a storybook marked by levity than a strait-laced, straight-faced textbook *per se*, I have not strived, much less contrived, to craft the language in a way that imparts a pedagogical halo to my writing. 不过,话说回来,对于学语言的学生而言,这本书不能噱头有余,干货不足,所以我特意注入一些养分,埋下一些彩蛋,譬如针对汉语成语、英语句型和同义词的使用,本书将大量实例有机地融入故事的叙述中,达到不解而解、无师自通的目的,却又避免舍本逐末、一味堆砌。That said, I would hate to hear language students complaining about my book being all show and no substance in an academic sense. I have seen to it that this book does serve up an abundance of linguistic goodies.

These Easter Bunny treats include, among others, a generous helping of examples to illustrate how to use, in context, etymologically interesting canned phrases in Chinese (*chengyu*) and how the English language's highly serviceable syntactic malleability and deliciously rich synonymity can be exploited, not to dress up the narrative to the nines, but to liven it up.

鉴于本书的两类读者（学英语的中国人和英语国家学汉语的学生）需求不同，本书中文和英文的"语域"似乎不合拍，中文部分以平铺直叙为主，英文部分时不时会来点文绉绉的描述或抒怀。In view of the disparate needs of the two segments of the book's potential readership (namely, Chinese-speaking students of English and English-speaking students of Chinese), there is an observable 'incongruity' - for want of a better word - between the registers of the Chinese text and of the corresponding English text, the former tending towards linear oral narration and the latter frequently peppered with rhetorical devices, i.e. anomalous spikes on an otherwise nuanced curve of discourse. 但这种文体的差异并非刻意为之，而是"原生态"的，完全符合笔者用这两种语言讲故事的一贯风格。But this doesn't mean I have had to bend or twist my preferred style of storytelling. In fact, this apparent disparity in register is native to my habit as a bilingual raconteur.

开场白多啰嗦几句，为的是让读者了解我的良苦用心。好了，话痨季就此打住，请诸君听故事吧。Okay, enough of my preambular spiel, which I deem to be a necessary evil. I don't know about you, but I, for one, am glad it's over. Phew! This is where the story begins.

Leonoir and Gingerlet 伙伴行

缘起　Where the Idea Came From

大约二十年前就想为儿子写本书了，无奈罹患"拖延症"，直到今日才"大病初愈"，正所谓"心动不如行动"，说干就干，否则一直拖下去的话，永远也写不出来。For a good 20 years, I kept telling myself that I should write a book for my son. But I came down with a dreaded lurgy called *procrastination*. I've only just recovered from it. What's that saying? 'Better late than never.' That's true. I could do worse than start now, however late this now may be.

下笔前，我给自己出了道选择题。I had a choice when I was contemplating what to put in the book that I was going to write. 我可以编一个故事，安排几个虚构的人物（例如小威、小敏之类的），说说这些人的家长里短。I could make up a story that would feature a number of fictitious characters（by such names as Willie and Minnie）going about their lives in fabricated settings. 我也可以说说我自己的故事。Or I could tell the story of my own life. 我思前想后，踌躇良久，最后决定：还是说自己的故事吧。I turned it over and over in my mind. After much humming and hawing, I came to a decision: to tell my own story. 因此，这本书的内容，纯属杂七杂八的凡人小事，所述故事均本人亲身经历，跟漫提显要或疗伤宣泄的高大上"自传"扯不上关系，因为我既非名人亦非"牛人"，唯有自知之明。It was to be a compilation of petty anecdotes culled from an average joe's bag of real-life experience. It would *not* purport to be some high-brow autobiography replete with nonchalant name-dropping or therapeutic catharsis, which requires either sufficient celebrity/notoriety or, in the absence of same, sufficient hubris/vainglory. I have neither. That much I know.

与多数年届半百的同龄人一样，我的故事很多，若要塞到一本书里，不说别的，光是装订就会成问题，所以必须有所侧重。本书主要搜罗我和动物小伙伴们的故事,夹杂跑龙套的人类角色若干……哦,还时不时跑跑题。I have lived through half a century. Most people at my age would have tons of stories to tell about themselves. I am no exception. If I were to fit them all into one book, it would be nothing short of an oversized tome bursting at the seams. For this reason, I think I'm better off focusing on stories of me and a motley crew of animal pals for now, supported by an eclectic lineup of human cameos... drifting inadvertently to unpremeditated tangential topics from time to time. 但无论跑题跑得多远,有个原则不会改变:书中每一个故事,以及每个故事的每个细节,都真实不虚,绝无添油加醋之处,记忆力远在我之上的母亲,还对这些细节一一确认、更正、补充了。Drifting notwithstanding, I am proud to vouch for the veracity of each and every story related in this book, down to minute details, all of which have been double-checked and verified by someone blessed with an eidetic memory, i.e. my mother. 窃以为,真实的故事更有感染力,天花乱坠只是过眼浮云。Personally, I find more charm in a true story faithfully told than in some embellished half-truths rattling with bells and whistles *ad nauseam*.

Leonoir and Gingerlet 伙伴行

我的根　Familial Context

父亲季之源是崇明人。崇明位于长江口，是一个由长江上游带来的泥沙堆积而成的小岛（故名冲积岛），离上海近，归上海管。My father, JI Zhiyuan, was born and bred in Chongming. Chongming is an 'alluvial' island (i.e. one formed by water-borne sediments from upstream) in the estuary of the Yangtze. It is very close to Shanghai and is considered part of Greater Shanghai.

跟别人提起我的籍贯，我通常这么说：就是那个岛，背靠上海滩，坐守长江口，远看像一条绿色的缎带，是中国第三大岛。When I try to explain to people where my father was born, Most of the time I would say, "You know, that island near Shanghai, in the river mouth of the Yangtze. From a distance, it looks like a green sash. It's China's third largest island."

听我对中国岛屿的概况如数家珍，听者往往若有所思，然后问我：中国的第一大岛和第二大岛又是哪两个呢？Since I've mentioned the size ranking of Chinese islands, many would stop and think, then ask: 'Which two islands are bigger than Chongming then?'

答案是：台湾岛和海南岛，老大、老二。I would say, 'Taiwan and Hainan, in that order.'

台湾同胞听了，可能先愣一下，因为他们对台湾"只是"中国第一大岛这样的概念不太习惯，但这毕竟是不争的事实，所以恼也不是，怒也不是，只能客气而勉强地笑笑，"嗯嗯"两声敷衍过去。If the person I am talking to is from Taiwan and the idea that Taiwan is *just* an island of China (and the biggest island, no less - oh wow!) is a little alien to them, they might freeze for a split second and then, slightly flustered or majorly peeved, put on a polite or forced smile while making some non-committal noises roughly equivalent to 'uh-huh'.

内地同胞（如果他们上地理课时脑子开小差，但依稀仿佛有点印象的话）听了，也许灵光一现："哦，对哦！"A mainlander (if he or she slept through their geography lessons at school, but has read about it in some obscure social media post) would suddenly see the light: 'Oh, yeah.'

对中国地理和政治一窍不通的老外听了，往往会作恍然大悟状："啊，原来如此。真有意思！"A foreigner who doesn't know the first thing about China's geopolitical complexity would say, 'Hmm, I see. Fascinating.'

但倘若这位外国友人对中国的情况一知半解，他很可能会咧着嘴，意味深长地冲我笑笑，说："哈哈，没错！"甚至还会拍拍我的肩。If, however, this *lao wai* has some knowledge of China, chances are he or she would break into a knowing grin and say, 'Ha-ha, yes, of course', accompanied, possibly, by a pat on my shoulder.

我只在崇明岛生活过两年，当时我很小，但那两年里发生的事情，至今记忆犹新。I spent two years on that island in my early childhood, but I still remember to this day many of the things that happened in that period.

母亲钦萍是宜兴人。My mother, QIN Ping, was born in Yixing. 介绍宜兴，简单多了。如果对方问起宜兴在哪里，或者他们的表情显示他们正在脑海里搜索宜兴在中国版图上的位置，我就会给他们一个提示："紫砂茶壶……"对方十有八九就会接茬："哦，那个宜兴。"Yixing is much easier to explain. If I am asked where Yixing is, or when my interlocutor appears to be searching their mental map to 'geotag' the place by that name, I would drop a hint, like a virtual pin on the 'map': 'Purple clay teapots... ring a bell?' Nine times out of ten, ding... a light would flash on in their head: 'Oh, that Yixing.' 如果对方是老外，那就再补充一点细节吧："那个用泥巴做传统茶壶的城市，离上海不远。"If they are foreigners, a little more detail wouldn't hurt: 'The town where the classic clay tea sets are made, not too far from Shanghai.' 这点信息，

Leonoir and Gingerlet 伙 伴 行

想必足矣,因为如果他们连泥巴烧制的茶壶都不知道,那么再费口舌恐怕也是徒劳无功。That would be sufficient information for them. If they have never seen or even heard of the 'classic clay tea sets' from China, what good would any extra trivia do? 说实话,宜兴我没去过,挺惭愧的。Truth be known, I have never been to Yixing, I am embarrassed to admit. 不过我已经承诺自己了:有生之年肯定会去,绝不抱憾终身。But all is not lost: Visiting Yixing is definitely on my bucket list.

认识我的人多半以为我是南京"杆子"。I'm known to many of my friends as the 'chap from Nanjing'. 但那仅仅因为我生在南京,多年后又在那里上了大学。But that's only because I was born in Nanjing and, many years later, went to university in that city. 我在南京的经历,按下不表,至少本书暂且略过。I'll leave the me-and-Nanjing stories till later. In fact, I don't think I'll cover them in this book.

现在说说我长大的地方——江苏兴化。Moving on to where I grew up... it's a place called Xinghua. 所谓我"长大"的地方,就是我童年生活最久的地方。光阴荏苒十二载。By 'where I grew up', I mean the place where I spent the better part of my childhood. I lived there for 12 years in total.

兴化三部曲,分别是三岁前、五岁至十岁、十岁至十四岁。这三个阶段的轨迹,可比作钟摆,来回振荡:县城、乡下、县城。My life in Xing-hua can be divided into three phases: up to age three; five to 10; and 10 to 14. A dotted line that connects these phases would describe the trajectory of a pendulum swing: three years in the county town, five years in a village and four years back in the county town. 有心人或许会纳闷:"三岁至五岁呢? 人间蒸发了? 难不成被外星人拐走了?" An observant reader might be wondering: What happened to you age three to five? Where did you disappear to? Were you a victim of alien abduction? 当然不是,据说外星人绑架只是一种幻觉。那两年,我呆在父亲的老家崇明,上文提过的吧? No, I wasn't. (Apparently, alien abduction is just a figment of imagination.) I was in Chongming, my father's hometown. I

- 11 -

have already mentioned it, haven't I?

与父母合影。(摄影:钦群) With my parents.(photo by Qin Qun)

Leonoir and Gingerlet　伙伴行

遥远的记忆　**Earliest Memory**

　　三岁前的事情，我居然还能记得，很多人觉得不可思议。但记忆的碎片是散落的、模糊的，唯有一件事至今历历在目，对于一个三岁孩童而言，那是一件大事。Believe it or not, I do remember certain things that happened before I turned three. But such memories are hazy and scanty, except for one. The only thing from that period I do recall with inexplicable lucidity was a major event in my three-year-old life.

　　那一天，爸爸妈妈告诉我，有位好心的叔叔要带我进电影院看电影，只有一张票，他们就不进去了。This is what I remember: My parents had told me that a very nice uncle was going to take me into the cinema to see a film. There was only one ticket for me, so they could not join me. 之后，便来了一个白衣装束的男人，他把我抱了起来。爸爸妈妈叮嘱我好好看电影，话音刚落，那人就抱着我进了一所大房子。Then came a man dressed in white. He picked me up and held me in his arms. My parents told me to enjoy the film and the uncle carried me into the building.

　　他抱着我，走在一条长长的过道里。另一位同样身着白衣的叔叔迎面走来，他们相互点点头，那位叔叔一手握着一个白色的茶缸，另一只手里攥着一支蓝色的牙刷。With me in his arms, the uncle walked down a very long corridor. On the way, another uncle, also in white, passed us by. They nodded to each other. That man had a white mug in one hand and a blue toothbrush in the other.

　　记忆中的下一个场景，就是我平躺在"座位"上，面向天花板，天花板吊着个很大的圆盘，圆盘里镶嵌着一盏盏灯。The next scene I remember is inside the 'cinema'. I lay down on my 'seat' and found myself facing a big round plate hanging from the ceiling. The plate was studded with light bulbs. 我想不通：这电影院真奇怪！其它电影院都是坐

着看电影,这儿怎么躺着看? 其它电影院都是后面挂一盏灯,前面吊一块大帘子,我看的是帘子,这儿怎么净看灯了? I was confused: What a strange cinema this is! In the normal cinema, I would sit and watch. But here, I am lying on my back. In other cinemas, there is a single light at the back and a large piece of white cloth at the front. I would be looking at the cloth. But here, I am actually staring at the lights, many lights. 回忆至此,戛然而止。 That is the point where my recollection of that event baulks abruptly. 多年后,我跟父母提起这段回忆,他们证实,那是一所医院——南京儿童医院。当时我得了"小肠气",必须接受手术。为了让我乖乖地跟陌生叔叔走,他们便哄我,说是去看电影。 Many years later, when I mentioned that memory to my parents, they confirmed I had been in a children's hospital in Nanjing at the time, undergoing an operation. I had had a hernia in my lower abdomen that the doctor had to fix. They had told me a porky-pie about going to the cinema, so I wouldn't say no to a stranger taking me away. 而我躺在手术台上看到的灯,就是无影灯。 And what met my eyes while I was lying on the operating table was the shadowless lamp. 后来我在一部关于针刺麻醉的纪录片里看到了无影灯,跟我记忆里的那所"影院"里看见的一模一样。 Years later, when I finally got to see a real operating 'theatre' in a documentary about acupuncture-induced anaesthesia, the shadowless lamp on the screen looked just like the one I had seen in that unusual 'theatre'. 再后来发生了什么,我记不起来了。当年全身麻醉用的还是乙醚,我嗅一嗅就"不省人事"了,因此记忆出现了断层。 Ether was still being used for general anaesthesia when I was operated on. I sniffed it and conked out straight away. A memory fault line was thus formed. 那年,我三岁。 I was three.

　　絮叨至此,诸位看官,感受如何?兴致依旧,还是哈欠连天? How do you feel? So far so good? Not yawning, yet? 请稍安勿躁。本书绝非编年史式流水账,否则如何做到我所奢求的引人入胜呢?尽管我深信,真实的故事更有吸引力,但听故事的人要是提不起劲来,听着听着

Leonoir and Gingerlet 伙 伴 行

睡着了，你的故事再真实也没有用啊。Don't worry. I shall not let this chronological thread run through my writing; nor will I weigh it down with mundane minutiae of my life. Otherwise this would not be a page turner, which every storybook ought to be. Instead, it would be a dreary, monotone rigmarole that guarantees nothing but yawns aplenty. While I'm convinced that reality does *not* get in the way of a good yarn, tedium does, for sure.

出气筒小黄　Gingerlet, the Pushover

说起打哈欠,我想起我对家里那只猫下的"毒手"。每次他打哈欠,只要我在附近转悠,总归忍不住把一根手指探进他张得大大的嘴里。Speaking of yawning, I am reminded of what I used to do to my cat. Whenever my cat yawned, if I was around, I would stick a finger in his wide-open mouth. For me, the temptation was simply too great to resist. 他也是个爱享乐的主儿,打哈欠时,自然紧闭双眼(否则打得不够畅快),因此我的小动作,他是看不见的,直到嘴巴再次合拢时,舌尖顶着我的手指了,才吓一跳,忙不迭地用毛茸茸的舌头把我手指拱出去。You see, when he was performing a big yawn, he would invariably shut his eyes (that's a must if you want to have a sinfully decadent oxygen boost), which meant he couldn't see what I was doing, until he closed his mouth again and felt my finger in it. Startled, he would try to get my finger out of his mouth with frantic, reflexive pushes of his furry tongue.

后来,他就尽量不在我身边打哈欠了。偶尔,刚张开嘴,突然若有所悟,赶紧合上,幽幽地走开了。能把打了一半的哈欠煞住,也是一种了不起的功夫啊!As a result of that, my cat stopped yawning in my vicinity. Occasionally, he would catch himself as he was about to open his mouth, think for a second, decide to abort yawning and walk away. No mean feat that was.

看官可能会说:"啧啧,多可怜的猫咪!"'Poor cat!' you might lament.

其实,他之所以可怜,不光因为摊上个以骚扰他为乐的小主人。In fact, this cat friend of mine evokes pity not just because he had the misfortune of being a mischievous boy's pet. 他的狗伙伴"黑狮"最初对他也不太友善。虽然我们本来没指望他俩擦出什么火花四溅的兄弟情,但猫咪初来乍到,黑狮二话不说就动用了"灭火器",还是让我们大跌眼

Leonoir and Gingerlet 伙伴行

镜。His canine housemate, *Heishi* (Black Lion), wasn't exactly a doting big brother to him at the beginning either. Although we hadn't expected them to get on with each other like a house on fire, the use of a 'water cannon' by *Heishi* on the first day was the last thing we had expected. 罪过罪过,差点忘了,我家的猫叫小黄。您猜对了,黄色狸花猫是也。By the way, my cat had a very common name: *Xiaohuang* (Little Yellow). He was, you guessed it, a ginger tabby. (I shall call him Gingerlet in this book. Just to be fair to *Heishi*, I shall also give him a European name in the context of this book. From now on, his name shall be Leonoir.)

　　黑狮比小黄的资格老。可他连自己的"窝"都没有,更不用说正儿八经的"狗屋"了。他平时就趴在某个角落里打盹或歇息,天冷了,才领到一个蒲团,垫在身下。Leonoir had joined our family before Gingerlet did. Leonoir did not have a 'nest' of his own, still less a 'kennel'. He would sleep or lounge in a corner inside the house, unless it was too cold, in which case he had a cushion to sleep on. 那个年代"宠物狗"的标配大致如此,它们充其量只能在主人跟前讨些欢心,就物质条件而言,"宠"字实在谈不上,因为主人的生活一般来说也相当艰苦。That seems to be the standard setup for 'pet' dogs (underdogs, more like) in those days when their human owners were by and large living a fairly spartan, if not needy, life. Pets might get some 'petting', but hardly any pampering. 更何况,在当时的中国,家养的小动物除了陪伴主人外,往往还各自肩负着自己"养家糊口"的重任。In fact, besides keeping their owners company, most of the small domestic animals were also expected to perform certain *practical* functions that established their *raison d'être*. 譬如,猫可以抓老鼠或把它们吓跑(当地方言叫"辟鼠"),狗可以给主人看家,鸡和鸭呢? 它们可以下蛋,贴补家用。For example, cats could catch or deter rats; dogs could guard their owners' property. Chickens and ducks? Their eggs could be sold to supplement the family income. (这也情有可原,因为宠物在其它动物眼里很可能属于富贵阶级、特权阶层,

沐浴在人类的青睐和保护中,既然地位高贵、养尊处优,自然责任重大,不容推卸。What with their elevated status in the human world *vis-à-vis* their peers in the wild, their enjoyment of human affection and protection and their entitlement to sundry other privileges in the comfort of a home, it stands to reason - and to the logic of *noblesse oblige* - that pets had to hold up their end of the bargain by contributing to their owners' well-being, one way or another.）而猫咪似乎是当时人们唯一的宠爱对象,也许是因为它们柔,抱着舒服,它们弱,能勾起人类的保护欲,它们的嬉戏,能激发人类的童趣。所以,人类跟猫狗玩耍的方式和态度也不同:对狗比较"粗暴",对猫则比较轻柔。Any semblance of mollycoddling, however, tended to go to cats, possibly because they were more cuddly, their apparent vulnerability appealed to the protective instinct of human beings and/or their ludic ways tickled them in exactly the right place. Rough-and-tumble was reserved for dogs; cats were typically handled with kid gloves. 小黄到我家后,我爸就用一个旧"饭焐子",在里面铺上软布,给小黄做了一个很舒服的窝。That is why after Gingerlet was welcomed into our family, my father made a very 'cosy' bed out of an old rice cooker 'cosy' by lining it with soft fabrics.

黑狮觉得这个小不点儿刚进家门就如此受宠,太不像话,羡慕嫉妒恨顿时涌上心头。That was just too much for Leonoir. He felt overslaughed. He seethed with envy, jealousy and resentment, in that order.

黑狮毫不掩饰自己的情绪,没等到第二天,就给小黄来了一个下马威。Leonoir made no attempt to disguise his feelings. He did something nasty to put Gingerlet in his place on the very first day. 起初他只是在小黄的窝边嗅来嗅去,我以为他只是好奇,没太在意,谁知一不留神,他突然跳进新窝,边踩踏边快速转圈。我看见了,一边呵斥一边一个箭步冲过去,但为时晚矣!就在我赶到前,他已经以迅雷不及掩耳之势,在小黄的新居里撒了一泡尿,撒丫子跑了! I noticed he was sniffing round Gingerlet's bed and thought he was just being curious, no cause for alarm. When I wasn't looking his way, he jumped into the nest all of a sudden and ran in circles while stomping on the 'bedding'. I saw what he was doing, yelled at him and sprinted across the room. But it was too late: By the time I got there, he had peed, at an impressive speed, into Gingerlet's new bed and skedaddled!

蒙特维多的邂逅（外一则）
A Stalker in Montevideo（with a bonus picture）

　　既然说到阿猫阿狗，那我就玩个穿越，讲述2010年我在南美与一只跟踪犬邂逅的故事。

　　Since we are on the topic of cats and dogs, let's do a bit of time travel and fast forward to 2010, so I can recount my encounter with a South American canine stalker.

　　　　它在街上闲逛。我也是
　　　　那个城市叫蒙特维多，乌拉圭首都
　　　　估摸是只丧家犬，但并不落魄
　　　　我看了它一眼。它没注意到我

Since we are on the topic of cats and dogs, let's do a bit of time travel and fast forward to 2010, so I can recount my encounter with a South American canine stalker.

Leonoir and Gingerlet　伙 伴 行

我心想:这条狗,躯体所承载的灵魂会是怎样的？它又经历过什么？
在这个当下,在这个空间,它和我产生交集;
而之前,我们天涯相隔
(这个天边之城,我飞了22个小时才到,有同事飞了30个小时)

就在这时
它扭头看了我一眼
很友好地走过来
我继续闲逛,它尾随

大约一小时过去了
虽然我知道它不是为了乞食而跟着我
但我还是把随身带的、仅存的一块芝麻糕掰成两半
一半放在地上
它摇摇尾巴,走过来
嗅嗅
抬头向我致谢
但不吃。
于是,我严肃地对它说：
"你不能再跟着我了",
"我要走了"。
它继续摇尾,继续尾随

又过了一小时
我看到前方有个公车站,人很多
我就挤进人群
快速穿行
再疾行至路侧。
回头远远看着它
只见它挨个儿嗅着等车的人

有时还走到一些人的面前
抬头辨认……

我转身,走了

I saw this dog in Montevideo. I was being a tourist and the dog, a local wanderer.
It was probably a stray, but not the mangy type.
I noticed it before it did me.
When I first laid eyes on it, a thought came to my mind from nowhere: 'What kind of soul is encaged in this canine body? What has this soul experienced through all its incarnations, up to this point, where our paths, hitherto far apart, are crossing?' (I had had to fly 22 hours to get here. Some of my colleagues had been less lucky.)
Just then, the dog turned round and saw me.
Wagging its tail and flashing a smile, it came over to me.
We exchanged pleasantries, linguistic and otherwise.
I carried on roaming the streets; it followed.
It was persistent, and greeted my numerous verbal discouragements with more tail wagging and more of what is analogous to a sunny human smile.
After about an hour, I stopped. I snapped a sesame snap in two and placed one piece on the pavement. I ate the other piece.
It gave the snack a cursory sniff out of courtesy, looked up to me to acknowledge my generosity and then looked away. It sat down.
I decided this interaction, which was getting us nowhere, had to stop and a serious tête-à-tête
was in order: 'You cannot follow me any more. You must go home. I'm going home, too!'
It kept up its multi-purpose tail gesticulation programmed to express positive sentiments, while 'listening' to me, but roundly ignored my

Leonoir and Gingerlet 伙伴行

message.
The tailing continued.
Another hour or so elapsed. I saw a bus stop thronged with passengers waiting for a late bus. I had to do what I had to do...
Ten seconds later, I emerged from the far side of the crowd. I quickly crossed the frontage road and peeked back:
The same dog was sniffing round the feet of the passengers at the bus stop, one by one.
Now and then, it would stop and look up to perform facial identification...

I turned round and walked off.

顺便欣赏一下这幅"怡然观景图"。同一天,同一座城市,四处游荡时,不经意间一抬头…… *While I am at it, why don't I throw in this delightful picture? I was rambling along in the same city on the same day, when I casually looked up... and there it was, a languid canine onlooker!*

黑狮粉墨登场　Enter Leonoir

说完南美遇犬记，再折回来说说本书的主角：黑狮和小黄。After straying to a Montevideo stray, let me return to Leonoir and Gingerlet, protagonists of this book.

我母亲给黑狮起了个外号——"黑衣绅士"。因为他全身乌黑透亮，唯独胸口镶一朵白色，正面看很像穿黑西装、打白领结的潇洒绅士！My mother nicknamed Leonoir 'Dark-Suited Gentleman', because he was jet-black all over, save for a white patch on his chest resembling a white bow tie matching a sleek dark suit. 整体而言，这位"黑衣绅士"文

黑狮。Leonoir.

质彬彬,颇具绅士风范,只是对陌生人有点凶,对小黄也时不时欺负一番,兄弟阋墙谈不上,充其量是无聊或妒忌。This dark-suited gentleman was well-mannered, by and large, not unlike a respectable squire. But strangers would have preferred a little less hostility from him and a little less bullying would have made Gingerlet's life more agreeable (albeit less stimulating perhaps). The bullying part was motivated not so much by sibling rivalry turning nasty as by boredom or plain jealousy.

有一次,我爸的一位外地同事到我家做客。My father had a work associate who lived in another town. He came to visit one day. 黑狮一反常态,他老远看到那人,低吼了一声,呼地冲出去,一口咬住他的脚踝不放。The guest was still quite far from our house when Leonoir saw him. Then something unusual happened. With a guttural growl, Leonoir whizzed towards the guest like a flash and held one of his ankles between his teeth. 客人大叫,我立即出去喝止,但黑狮没有马上松口,他四脚用力撑住,死死拽住那人,不让这个疑似入侵者挣脱,同时口中恶狠狠的呜噜声不绝。The poor guy cried for help. I went to his rescue and yelled at Leonoir. But Leonoir did not let go of his ankle right away. He secured his bite while firmly pushing against the ground with all four legs, digging his heels in, so to speak, so the suspected intruder could not get away. The threatening growl continued. 他抬眼看着我,意思是:你真的信任此人吗? In the meantime, he looked up at me, seeking confirmation: 'Are you sure this person can be trusted?' 我用语言和眼神告诉他:"赶紧松开!"他这才松开。I said to him, both with words and with the glower in my eyes, 'Yes, let go of him, now!' He complied. 我骂他,让他快滚,他二话不说,低眉顺眼灰溜溜地走开了。As I was berating him and telling him to make himself scarce, he slunk off in silence, ears flopping down, eyes looking down, his tail between his legs. 送走客人后,我爸说:"这个人我的确不大喜欢,但黑狮怎么知道的呢?"Later, when the visitor had left, my father remarked, 'I don't really like this guy, but how could Leonoir possibly know that?' 他又说:"不过黑狮也不应

该一见着主人不喜欢的人就上去咬啊，这实在说不通，也太尴尬了。"
He continued, 'But just because I don't like someone doesn't mean our dog should bite them. That was so embarrassing.'

对陌生人目如鹰隼的黑狮，此刻眼神热切，他似乎知道我们正在说他，也察觉出是不带好气的。对此我们确信无疑。他使劲摇着尾巴，盯着我们，仿佛在说："嗯，我听话，不捣蛋。我看家护院全力以赴，因为我疼你们。"难道他真的听懂了我们褒扬他的具体内容吗？这个问题我们也无从解答。Leonoir, the eagle-eyed blitzing watchdog, was now eager-eyed as he listened attentively to my father's comment. He knew we were discussing him and was aware of the mood of the conversation. That much we knew for sure. He stared at us while wagging his tail with abandon, as if saying, 'Yes, I'm a good boy. Yes, I do try, because I love you.' Did he understand *exactly* what was said about him? The question defies a definitive answer.

但不管怎么说，每次一提起黑狮的名字，只要他在场，他马上就有反应。In fact, Leonoir was so sensitive to the sound of his name that whenever it came up in our conversation, he knew right away as long as he was within earshot.

那段日子，我们虽然住在兴化县城，但一家三口交谈时，用的却是一种以吴方言为主料、兴化县城和三泰方言为辅料的自创混合型家庭语体。Although we were living in the county town of Xinghua at the time, the language we spoke at home was a hybrid familial vernacular, combining elements of my parents' own dialects from their respective hometowns in Greater Shanghai, crossed with accents and usages of Xinghua and the Three Tai region. 且慢，何谓"三泰"？三泰是指泰州、泰兴、泰县（姜堰）。我们曾在兴化下属的戴南公社生活过五年，而戴南临近泰州，戴南人的口音更接近泰州方言，跟兴化县城的口音，有很大的差异。Hang on, Three Tai? What Three Tai? It refers to the region of Taizhou, Taixing and Taixian (aka Jiangyan). Within the administrative hierarchy, there was a commune (now called a 'township') subordinate

Leonoir and Gingerlet 伙 伴 行

to Xinghua, but located quite far from Xinghua's county seat. This commune, Dainan, borders the city of Taizhou. People in Dainan and Taizhou speak more or less the same dialect, quite distinct from that of Xinghua proper. We had once lived in Dainan for five years. 无论是兴化话还是以吴语系为主的季家方言，都没有卷舌音，"狮"的发音与"丝"无异。In both Xinghua dialect and the vernacular of the Ji's, retroflexed (or cacuminal, i.e. with the tip of the tongue curled up towards the hard palate) consonants are absent, so zh, ch and sh are pronounced as alveolar affricates (dz and ts) and the lingua-alveolar fricative (s). I think I need to expand on this a little *en passant*, for the benefit of learners like my son: In *Putonghua* (Mandarin Chinese), retroflexed consonants, zh, ch and sh, sound like dj, ch and sh in English, except that they are 'drier'. This dryness is achieved by placing the tip of the tongue in a slightly different place on the hard palate. For example, in English, ch is pronounced with the upper side of the tongue's front part pressed against the mid part of the hard palate. Air is then pushed through a relatively large area of contact between the tongue and the hard palate. But in *Putonghua*, the ch sound is created by making the very tip of the tongue touch the borderline between the hard palate and the soft palate. Air passes through a much smaller area of contact between the tip of the tongue and the ceiling of the oral cavity. That explains why some native speakers of *Putonghua* pronounce the 'ch' in 'China' much too 'dry'. As I said earlier, my parents and I, when speaking at home, replaced 'zh', 'ch' and 'sh' with 'dz', 'ts' and 's'. 因此，我每回喊黑狮，只需微启双唇发出"丝"音即可，哪怕相隔几十米，他也会立即跑过来，用眼神试探性地问："主人，您找我？" That means when I wanted to have Leonoir's attention, all I needed to do was make an 's' sound (corresponding to the 'sh' in his name Heishi, Black Lion). He would come running up to me from dozens of yards away and enquire with his eyes: 'Master, anything I can do for you?'

- 27 -

重逢，情难抑　The Unbearable Happiness of Reuniting

但是，"咝"这个音有个很大的缺陷：传得还是不够远。But 's' had a major drawback: It wouldn't travel very far. 假设隔着一里地，我要召唤他过来，怎么办？So, if we were hundreds of yards apart and I wanted to beckon him over, what would I do? 答：我就得吹口哨！The answer: I would whistle!

那时候我家住在水产养殖场（我父亲是水产工程师），我在兴化红卫中学（后恢复其原名"昭阳中学"）上初中，每天放学回家要走四十五分钟，途经一条宽宽的公路。At that time, our home was on a fish farm (my father being an aquaculture specialist and fish breeder) and I was attending the county's Hongwei School at the junior secondary level. (Hongwei means Red Guard. Years later, it reverted to its former name Zhaoyang, 'Bright Sun', after Xinghua's ancient name.) My 45-minute walk home every day included a long trek on an open highway. 夏天、无风、无云、烈日炎炎，那条公路空旷极了，两边没有树，所以没有树荫，阳光把空气炙烤到三十八、三十九度，我的视线开始模糊：一匹白马从天而降，在被烤软的柏油路面上，马蹄得得，马鬃飘飘，像一道闪电，把我从苦难中救出，送到目的地。By 'open', I mean the highway had no shade whatsoever, either from trees or manmade structures. On cloudless, windless summer days, when the searing sun toasted air temperatures to high 30s, that highway provided the setting for one of my enduring fantasies: that a white steed would turn up from nowhere and carry me home or to school with lightning speed and great panache, its luxuriant mane streaming in the wind, its hooves clattering on the blistering tarmac… 到家前的最后一段，是连片鱼塘的堤坝构成的一条泥路，只要不下雨，还是挺好走的。路也不算窄，一头水牛和一个行人可以并排走过；也不短，有一里多。我家屋子跟这条路隔着一个鱼塘，大约30米。Lying

Leonoir and Gingerlet 伙 伴 行

between the highway and our house was the 'last mile' - a dirt road, a stretch of berm bordering several fish ponds bookended by more fish ponds. Our house was set back from this road by about 30 yards. It wasn't a bad road when it was not raining. Hundreds of yards long, it was broad enough to accommodate a pedestrian and a buffalo passing each other. 路的一侧是河岸，河水流向哪里，是个未解之谜；另一侧就是一溜方形的鱼塘，这些鱼塘我倒是颇知一二，黑狮和小黄的很多故事，都是在这一带演绎的。On one side of the road was a river. I did not, and do not, know where the river led to. On the other side were the fish ponds, lined up like an ice cube tray. I was very familiar with those ponds. It was there that most of my reminiscences featuring Leonoir and Gingerlet played out. 至于那条河，我曾在小伙伴的教唆下，在河里学游泳，但我终究也没学会，至今依然是一只"旱鸭子"。The river was where I took a shot

兴化，六十年代。有故事的鱼塘。(摄影：单家容) *Xinghua, 1960s. Fish ponds, with many a tale to tell. (Photo by Jiarong Shan)*

at learning to swim, egged on by my buddies, human buddies. But I didn't become a swimmer in that river after all. I'm like that famous navy cadet who, upon graduation, was advised by his dejected swimming instructor: 'In the event of a shipwreck, Tom, just sink to the bottom and *walk* to the shore!'

我上学时，走完鱼塘路，经过公路旁的一家早点铺子，我每天的早饭就在那儿买。When I went to school in the morning, I would buy my breakfast from a takeaway at the junction between the embankment road and the highway. 我的早饭是两根"麻团"，每根8分钱，2两粮票，所以我每天早上要吞食4两碳水化合物，而且滴水不进。My breakfast consisted of just two pieces of *matuan* - sesame seed-coated deep-fried glutinous rice balls with a sweet filling (quite a mouthful, compared to the bisyllabic Chinese name - *matuan*). For each, I would pay eight cents, plus 3.5 ounces' worth of ration stamps (food being rationed in China in those days). That means I would devour seven ounces of pure carbs every morning, and no fluid whatsoever. "麻团"，顾名思义是球状的，但我却用"根"作量词，奇怪吧？原因是，那家店不知为何，喜欢把麻团做成擀面杖形状，所以我们家把它称作"麻棍"。The reason I've interrupted the contextual flow and brought up the topic of *matuan* is because they were quite unusual. They were not spherical as the word *tuan* suggests. For some reason, they were shaped more like a rolling pin, an idiosyncrasy of that particular bakery. We jokingly called them *magun* (pronounced *maa gooen*, meaning 'sesame rods'). 有一天，我照例一手一根麻棍，边走边嚼，两个路过的外地人看到了，觉得非常滑稽，其中一人说："快看那个小鬼，那么瘦，吃那么多！" One day I was going about my breakfast routine, that is, holding one *magun* in each hand, walking and noshing at the same time, when two passers-by noticed me. One of them marvelled at my feat and remarked in a dialect I could not identify, 'Look at that little fella, he certainly eats a lot for his skinny body!' 有一年，芝麻歉收，这爿店断了货源，该有芝麻的，芝麻都不见了，麻棍也不"麻"了，只剩

Leonoir and Gingerlet　伙伴行

下"光棍"！One year, after a bad harvest of sesame, the bakery ran out of this essential ingredient. It disappeared from products like *magun*. What do you call a sesame rod minus the sesame? That would be a *guanggun*. Yes, you guessed it: a naked rod!

　　学校下午四点一刻放学，我到家大约五点。School finished at a quarter past four and I would get home around five. 据母亲说，每天快到五点时，黑狮总会在屋前出现，而之前他或许在屋子里打盹，或许在池塘边跟哥们儿玩耍，但一旦到了我快到家的点儿，他就立马现身，比瑞士手表还准。According to my mother, shortly before five o'clock each day, Leonoir would appear in front of the house. He might have been sleeping at home or playing with his chums round the fish ponds prior to that, but when I was about to get home, he would suddenly turn up, with uncanny punctuality. 他两眼紧盯着远方的河堤小道，原本就直溜溜的耳朵竖得更直。他还不忘瞟母亲一两眼，嗓子眼里发出"咝咝"的声音，大概是说："嗯，嗯，少爷快回家了！我要淡定，要淡定！" He would fix his gaze on the path leading up to the berm and cock his already upstanding ears. He would cast a side-glance or two at my mother while throating a hissing sound, meaning, 'Yes, I know, young master is on his way home! I mustn't get too excited, no, I mustn't.'

　　那时，依然在一里多开外的我，已经踏上那条泥路。我轻轻吹一声口哨，就一声，轻轻的。By then, I had set foot on that dirt road, hundreds of yards away. I would whistle. Softly. Just once.

　　我母亲听力超常，估计特异功能也不过如此。但即便耳朵这么尖，也只能勉强听到从远处飘来的若有若无的那声口哨，有时甚至怀疑是自己的幻觉。黑狮却肯定听见了。母亲说，每当此时，黑狮就突然开始"发神经"，先是在原地团团转，像陀螺，又像憋足了劲的发条玩具。几秒钟后，箭在弦上，不得不发，这陀螺就会沿着圆弧的切线，朝着鱼塘路的方向飙射出去。My mother has extraordinary hearing, bordering on the supernatural, but even sharp ears like hers had to strain and struggle to pick up the hushed decibels of my whistle at that distance. She wasn't even sure that she had actually heard it. But Leonoir was. She would see him suddenly turning into, in her words, an 'unhinged lunatic' or a 'spinning top', like a wind-up toy releasing momentum or a discus thrower building momentum. Seconds later, this top would go off at a tangent (literally) and hurl itself (not the discus) in the direction of the road.

与此同时，我继续前行，眼睛却盯着路的尽头。I would continue walking, all the while keeping my eyes on the far end of the road. 几秒钟后，地平线上腾起一团灰尘，一个"黑绒线球"，由小渐大，冲着我飞速滚来。Seconds later, a cloud of dust would appear on the horizon. A black furry blob would come into view and start growing in size while careering towards me. 倘若是在电影里，大概会呈现如下声光色交融的一幕：镜头缓缓拉近，给奔跑的黑狮一个大特写，他的舌头耷拉着、他的肚皮贴着地面，四条短腿飞速蹬地，四下尘土飞扬，激昂的音乐声（类似二胡曲《赛马》渐起，一节节推向高潮。If we transposed this scene onto the silver screen, this would be what we see and hear: Leonoir gallops forward in slow motion, his tongue lolled out, his tummy skimming the ground, his image obscured by the dust he is kicking up with his short, fast-moving legs. Some rousing music (like the theme of Chariots of Fire) fades in and builds up to a crescendo. 这就是我当时的感觉，只是没有音乐，而我的口哨声早已消逝在空气中。That's exactly what it was like on that road in that moment, minus the music or any other sound, as my whistle had travelled far out of earshot by then. 随即，黑狮冲到我面前，在三米开外就急不可耐地纵身一跃，在空中划出一条漂亮的弧线，扑进我的怀中。Before long, Leonoir would reach the finishing line, i.e. about three yards in front of me. Sprinting any further would have taken too much of his time, in his estimation. So, with a mighty push of his hind legs, Leonoir would be airborne… and lunge into my arms.

猜猜我当时的反应？像广告或者电影里那样，抱住热情洋溢的黑狮，让他用淌着"哈喇子"的舌头劈头盖脸猛舔一气？没门儿！在黑狮

Leonoir and Gingerlet 伙伴行

纵身跃起尚未与我亲密接触的瞬间,说时迟那时快,我先接住他的前腿,再像魔术师两手交叉抖搂手帕反面那样,干净利落地给他来个向后转,让他面朝前方。这个动作的关键是时机的把握,不容闪失!

Guess what I would do now? Would I reciprocate Leonoir's exuberant 'outpourings' with a bear hug or even by accepting a slobbering smooch from him, like what you see in films and TV commercials? No way! As he pounced on me, I would catch his front legs while he was still in the air and flip him round in one clean move (in the fashion of a magician crossing his hands to show the reverse side of his handkerchief), so he would face the other way. I would accomplish that in a fraction of a second. Timing was the name of the game and I couldn't afford to miss. 我之所以如此煞风景,是因为兴奋过度的黑狮已经小便失禁了,在期盼已久的重逢即将兑现的瞬间,情不自禁地突然"一泻如注",而我那个动作,就是为了让他把尿飙向空中,而不是把我淋成一只"落汤鸡"!

Why was I being such a party pooper? Because Leonoir would be so excited by now that bladder control had given way to incontinence. Involuntarily, he would relax a certain part of his body all of a sudden upon the reunion that he had so looked forward to. Turning him away would spare myself a shower of liquid 'outpouring'!

总而言之,每天放学后我和黑狮的重聚,就是一束闪电、两条弧线:始于一束黑色闪电掠过尘土飞扬的道路,黑狮纵身一跃划出的是第一条弧线,他小便失禁射向空中的是第二条弧线。To recap, my daily homecoming encounter with Leonoir boils down to a flash of black lightning tearing along a dusty road, ending in two arcs: the arc drawn by his body as he catapulted himself into the air towards my arms and the other arc a wee-wee-leak from this sprinter in hyper mode, shot into the air.

大胃王小猫　The Kitten That Eats Like a Pig

当主人与狗轰轰烈烈演绎这出"尿不湿"二人转的同时,小黄在哪儿?在忙什么呢?While that one-man-and-his-dog show was going on, 'overflowing' with boisterous, pee-jerking melodrama, where was Gingerlet? And what was he up to? 答案是:他也没闲着,他在捉鱼,而且是徒手捉鱼!The answer: He was busy too, catching fish. And doing so with bare paws!

"小黄"这个名字里的"小"字,有点误导。刚来我家时,他确实挺小的,巴掌大小。The name Gingerlet is something of a misnomer. Yes, he was indeed quite small, the size of a palm, when he first came to our house. 记得那天到了吃午饭的时间,一家三口从不同的地方回家吃饭,父亲回来得稍晚,他到家时饭菜已经摆上桌了。It was lunchtime. I came home from school and my parents, from their respective work 'units'. Father was late. By the time he got home, food was already on the table. 他进来时,没什么异常,只是表情似笑非笑,神秘兮兮的。As he stepped through the door, he had a mysterious look on his face, like a suppressed smile. Everything else about him seemed normal. 他一言不发,径直走到桌边,一只手漫不经心地搁在桌上——我和母亲不约而同地惊呼一声,一只"袖珍"猫,从他的衣袖里慢悠悠地爬了出来。Without a word, he walked up to the table and casually placed one hand on it... Mother and I gasped at the same time: A pocket-sized (or 'sleeve-sized') baby kitten slowly crawled out of his sleeve. 从那天起,每次吃饭,小黄都趴在父亲的脖子上,探着小脑袋,父亲自己吃一筷子,喂他一筷子。他成了父亲的天然毛围脖儿。From that day on, whenever we ate, Gingerlet would drape himself on the back of my father's neck, in the fashion of a fur scarf, his tiny head reaching down. Father would alternate between chopsticking food into his own mouth and letting Gingerlet eat

Leonoir and Gingerlet 伙伴行

from his chopsticks. 对这样的"吃相",母亲很不满,但除了唠叨几句"玩物丧志",也没怎么干涉。Mother was miffed at such reprehensible table manners, but her intervention went little beyond pitching a few admonitory pearls of wisdom at him. 'Indulgence in playthings is, alas, the bane of a man's spirit' was one of them.

可是没过多久,小黄就不"小"了。But Gingerlet ceased to be a kitten-'let' before long. 他最大的特点是:吃嘛嘛香,食量惊人! He was an outstanding cat for his outstanding appetite.

而"好吃"这个特征又和他的同类有太多格格不入之处。His voracious craving for food was unusual in many ways against the behavioural baseline of domestic cats. 例如,他在家里的主食是粥,大量的白粥。For example, plain rice congee was his bread and butter at home, and he would eat copious amounts of it. 如果你不理解,问他:"你可是猫啊,白粥有啥好吃的?"他可能觉得你的问题更加费解:"白粥有啥不好吃的?" If you find it incomprehensible and ask him, 'Why do you, a cat, like congee?' he might find your question more incomprehensible and ask you back, 'What's not to like?' 他一旦开吃,便义无反顾,勇往直前。我在后面瞥见他的肚皮撑得越来越鼓,叫停,他不停,呼哧呼哧一个劲儿地狼吞虎咽,直到我实在看不下去了,只能从后面拽他的后腿,把他和他的宝贝粥碗强行拆散。Once he started eating congee, there was no stopping him. I could see his tummy filling out and turning into the shape of a drum. Convinced that he would get sick from the binge, I would order him to cease and desist, only to be ignored by him. He would carry on, noisily wolfing down the congee with happy abandon. In the end, I would have no choice but to yank him away from his congee bowl by tugging at his hind legs. 好在小黄脾气好,被拉开后,只是恋恋不舍地再看一眼碗里的剩粥,然后乖乖地走到一边"饭后洗脸"。换作其他猫,吃饭的时候遭到打扰,那可是犯了大忌,一定怒发冲冠,气咻咻跟你撕破脸皮(有时真的会撕破你的脸皮)。Gingerlet was so good-natured that he would take one last longing look at what remained in his congee bowl and meekly walk away to embark on his postprandial grooming ritual. Another cat would have bridled and bristled, hissed and huffed, or even snarled and scratched, if I had disturbed its eating.

小黄胃口超好，还体现在另一个方面。That was not all that made him a true glutton. 猫吃饭时，一般都是用布满倒刺的舌头把食物"舔"到嘴里，猫舌头的滞留功能很强，连水都可以轻弹舌尖"刷刷"作声收罗到嘴里。An average cat typically *laps up* what is on offer, which means it relies on its spiny tongue to *lick* the food into its mouth, morsel by bite-sized morsel. The retaining function of a cat's tongue is so effective that it can even catch liquid and flick it into the mouth in small, swift, continual moves. 但小黄不同，他是直接张开嘴，把干湿食物或饮料"铲"进嘴里，再囫囵吞下，酣畅淋漓。But Gingerlet was different in that his definition of eating was opening his mouth, shovelling the food in with his jaws (or quaffing it, if it was fluid or semi-fluid, like congee) and gulping it down. Nice and easy, and thoroughly satisfying.

我替小黄称过体重，在他成长的某个阶段，半个月内，他就从一只小猫崽，长成了一只4.5公斤的大猫！I weighed him from time to time. At one stage, in a space of a fortnight, the teensy kitten grew into a 10-pound giant! 有位邻居观察了一阵子后，断定小黄是家猫和"土豹"杂交的混血儿。父亲说，当地人所谓的土豹，就是从来没有做过家猫的、体型偏大的野猫。A neighbour of ours, having observed Gingerlet for some time, offered his taxonomical conclusion: Gingerlet is a cross between a domestic cat and a local 'leopard'. Father later explained that by leopard, the neighbour was referring to one of those larger feral cats in the wild. 当时我心想，也许是猞猁之类的。总之，一想到自己养的是一只半野的"兽"，我就情不自禁得意起来！I thought to myself: Maybe Gingerlet's parent is a lynx or some such thing. Whatever it was, it did not worry me. Instead, the thought that my buddy was a semi-wild 'beast' gave me goosebumps.

邻居的判断应该没错，小黄后来的某些行为，证明了他肯定不是普通家猫。The neighbour's verdict was probably right. It was borne out by Gingerlet's subsequent behaviour, which was very untypical of an average homebody.

小黄在家几乎只吃干饭和稀饭,偶尔大口地"吞喝"白开水。At home, Gingerlet was only interested in rice, either steamed rice or congee. He might take 'swigs' of boiled water from his bowl occasionally, but that's about it. 这应该跟他从小睡在饭焐子里关系不大。This probably had little to do with the fact that he had been sleeping in a rice cooker cosy from a young age. 那么他从哪儿摄取蛋白质呢？反正不是老鼠（有关老鼠，以后再说）。But protein - where did he get his protein from? No, not from rats (rats will be discussed in detail a little later). 还没想起来吗？他有空爪捉鱼的本领。Don't you remember? He could catch fish with bare paws.

自给自足的黄渔翁 The Self-Sufficient Fishercat

我只要全天在家,就会目睹小黄急匆匆地赶回家,嘴里叼着一条或大或小的鱼。起初我以为是死鱼,不知他从哪里捡回来的,但仔细一看,都是活蹦乱跳的,只不过被他死死咬住,蹦跳不起来,只能在"虎口"里费力地扭动。Whenever I was home all day, I would see Gingerlet rushing home with a fish in his mouth at some point. The size of the fish varied. Initially I thought they were dead fish that he had picked up from somewhere. But a closer examination revealed that they were all alive and kicking. Well, not exactly kicking... His bite was so strong they could manage little more than a feeble wriggle.

小黄。*Gingerlet*.

Leonoir and Gingerlet　伙伴行

我第一次看到这个情景时,曾厉声厉色地问他:"好啊你!快交代,这是从哪家偷来的?" The first time it happened, I interrogated him, stern-voiced and stone-faced: 'I don't believe this. Where did you steal it from? You'd better come clean.' 他衔着还在挣扎的鱼,停下脚步,抬起湿漉漉的小脸,茫然地看着我,表示不知所云。 The writhing prey still in his mouth, he stopped and looked up. 'Puzzled' is what I saw branded across his forehead. Obviously my question went straight over his head. 然后他继续前行,找个角落,大嚼起来。 He then moved on, found a corner in the house and started chomping away.

后来我和父母都分别目睹了黄大侠捉鱼的场面。 My parents and I later witnessed our 'king fisher' in action on different occasions. 被我撞见的几次,小黄都是耐心地坐在鱼塘边,纹丝不动,眼睛盯着水下的动静,等一条倒霉的鱼游过来时,他就闪电般出手,在水中一捞,得手后随即把鱼塞进嘴里,扭头就往家里跑。整个过程也就一两秒,鱼塘波澜不惊。 The few times I had the pleasure of catching Gingerlet *in flagrante delicto*, I saw the following: He planted himself at the water's edge of a fish pond, in statuesque stillness. His steady gaze penetrated the water to observe the goings-on beneath the surface. When an unlucky fish swam into his ambush, he stuck one paw out, quicker than a spring-loaded punching fist used by boxers, scooped the stunned fish out of water and stuffed it in his mouth, before turning round and dashing home. The whole sequence was over in a couple of seconds. His moves were so fast and so light the pond was unruffled, as if nothing had happened.

母亲有幸看到了另外一幕,更加精彩。 But that display of fishing skills paled in comparison to what my mother witnessed. 某个鱼塘的鱼中了几次埋伏后,吃一堑长一智,不在水边游荡了,而是集中在鱼塘的中央吃喝玩乐,让不识水性的天敌小黄干着急。 The fish that populated one particular pond frequented by Gingerlet learnt their lessons and gave the shores a wide berth. They decided they had a better chance of survival if they stayed round the centre of the pond, outside the striking

- 39 -

range of their exterminator, who was as much a non-swimmer as his young master. 那个鱼塘里常年漂浮着一些圆木，父亲说是某类木材的预处理工序，这个工序当地人称作"沉水"。Fish were not the only inhabitants of that pond. There were always some large logs floating on the surface. Soaking in water was part of the pretreatment for certain types of timber, according to my father. 有一天，母亲远远看到小黄端坐在鱼塘中央的一根圆木上，显然他是在圆木漂到水边时跳上去的，后来圆木又随风漂到了鱼塘中央，上船容易下船难，小黄被困在了湖心。One day, my mother stumbled upon a most extraordinary scene: Gingerlet was sitting on a log in the middle of the pond. He had, by the looks of it, jumped onto the log when it was close to shore, before it drifted away. Now he was marooned in that makeshift 'canoe', up the creek without a

小黄观鱼，不怀好意。Gingerlet admires the fish, with an ulterior motive.

paddle, quite literally. 母亲急了，赶紧开动脑筋琢磨该怎么救小黄。Mother told herself not to panic. She put on her thinking cap: How could I get Gingerlet out of this fine mess? 这时她定睛一看，咦，小黄怎么不叫也不慌呢？She took a closer look, only to find Gingerlet calm and unflustered. He wasn't even meowing for help. 'That's odd,' she thought. 再一看，她明白了：小黄放弃了捞鱼，改为钓鱼了，他用尾巴钓鱼！She looked again and saw what was really going on: Gingerlet had changed his *modus operandi* from harpooning (with his nailed paws) to angling (with his tail)! 从鱼的角度来看，硕大的圆木在水面晃晃悠悠地漂来漂去，恐怖极了，所以它们敬而远之，小黄必须把自己的黄白双色尾巴垂入水中，才能诱引它们进入捞鱼半径。The fish had thought it wise to steer well clear of those huge logs drifting erratically on the surface and casting ominous shadows onto the bottom of the pond. To lure them into his radius of action, Gingerlet needed a bait. And what better bait than his own wriggly, fluffy, gaily coloured tail?

一旦鱼儿"咬钩"，小黄的后续动作就和我之前看到的场景大同小异了，唯一的区别是，他得委屈自己，只能在湖心"独木舟"上就地用餐。When a fish came over to nibble at the bait, all Gingerlet needed to do was repeat his harpooning routine, the only difference being that once he had caught his prey, he had to rough it and picnic on his royal float, not in the comfort of his home. 吃完，"船"也自行靠岸了，他怡然自得，优雅地轻跃上岸，用眼神向我母亲打了个招呼，迤逦而行，回家洗脸喝粥去了。At the end of his 'fish-*on*-chips' meal, the log had drifted back to shore. An effortless leap sent him back to *terra firma* with poise and precision. He gathered himself, greeted my mother with an *oh-there-you-are* look and started trotting homeward to freshen up and to have his seconds - a bowl of congee.

智力测验　IQ Test

有时，小黄叼着猎物回家时，大门关着，他就得钻窗户，因为嘴里叼着东西，无法叫门，何况他也等不及了。Sometimes, the front door was closed when Gingerlet came home with his victim. He had to come in through the window, because he couldn't meow for our attention when he had something in his mouth and this was not the time for patience as far as he was concerned. 铁窗花的空隙其实够大，他那柔韧的身躯完全可以自如地出入，但如果嘴里横叼着一条鱼，鱼的长度就超出两根铁条之间的宽度了。The gaps in the window grille were wide enough for his supple, collapsible body to get in and out with ease. But those gaps became impassable when he had a fish in his mouth. 这种情况考验的是小黄的智力。不过不打紧，小黄不仅四肢发达，头脑也是一流的。That is when Gingerlet's intellect was put to the test. He did, however, prove to be as brainy as he was brawny. 有一天，我正在屋里做作业（或者在发呆），突然，窗台上冒出小黄的脑袋，口里衔着条鱼，前爪紧紧扒住窗台。显然，对他来说，负重跳高易如反掌。One day, I was doing my homework or just staring into space when I suddenly saw Gingerlet's head popping up from the windowsill, with a fish in his mouth, of course. His front claws dug into the ledge to secure his foothold. Imagine, if you will, high jump with sandbags strapped to your legs. An equivalent of that was, evidently, anything but a 'tall order' for Gingerlet. 他顾不上跟我打招呼，对准铁窗花的某个空隙，毫不犹豫直冲进来。Without much ado, without even greeting his master, he aimed at a gap in the grille and made a lunge. "砰"的一声，他碰壁了，鱼身太长，进不来。Bang! He was beaten back by the grille. The fish was too long. 他不甘心，再试一次。"砰"！又失败了。The doughty fish runner tried again. Bang! And again he failed. 每次撞上铁条时，他都会先闭一下眼睛，再皱一下眉头，不是因

挫败而沮丧，估计是眼冒金星吧。Each time he hit and got repelled by the iron bars, he scowled and squinted, not out of frustration, but because the impact stunned him momentarily and made he see stars. Or so I surmised.

但他不会跟自己过不去，傻乎乎地试第三次。他停下来，迅速打量一下格栅，再把脑袋转90度，这样鱼就呈垂直态，跟铁条平行，他就带着猎物顺顺当当进来了。But he wasn't ready to humiliate himself with a third failure. Instead, he stopped, made a quick visual survey of the grille and *rotated his head 90 degrees*, so the fish became vertical, parallel to the bars. That's how he got into the house, with his prey in one piece.

此后，他每次这样回家，只要试一次就行了。如果鱼太长，他就以自己的脑袋为轴心，以鱼头、鱼尾为时针和分针，从3点40分（因为鱼头、鱼尾稍稍下垂）拨到6点整，就能将路障一举排除。From then on, whenever he needed to negotiate the window like this, he would repeat the trial-and-error approach once. If the fish proved to be too long, he would pivot his head and turn the fish from 3:40 (its head and tail pointing downwards slightly) to 6 o'clock... *et voila*, problem solved!

护鱼卫士　**The Catcher Watcher**

说到猫和鱼，让我插播我四岁那年在崇明发生的一件事。这件事我自己是不记得了，是我祖母告诉我母亲的，婆媳俩都觉得那个场景喜感十足。Speaking of cat and fish, please allow me to interpose a little flashback to when I was four. I was in Chongming. I cannot recall that particular incident. It was recounted by my grandmother on my father's side. She and her daughter-in-law, i.e. my own mother, both thought it hilarious, at my expense.

有一天，我们准备中午吃鱼。奶奶把几条鱼清洗完毕后，放进一只大碗，大碗再搁在水缸上面。One day, we were going to have fish for lunch. Gran cleaned the fish and put them in a large bowl, which was then placed on top of the water vat (a huge earthen container for storing drinking water purified with potash alum). 这样离地面有一定的高度，猫从地面够不着，即便能跳上去，动静又太大，家里有人时，她不敢。This was a safety precaution to keep the fish out of her cat's reach. Gaining access to the fish would require a big jump on the cat's part and it would be difficult not to be noticed when we were around. 这时奶奶发现酱油用完了，于是对我说："我去打酱油，你看好鱼，别让猫吃了。" At that point, Gran noticed she had run out of soy sauce, which was indispensable for the fish dish, so she said to me, 'I'm going to get some soy sauce. Keep an eye on the fish. Make sure the cat doesn't get to it.' 作为猫的主人，奶奶当然对猫的弹跳力了如指掌，她很清楚，水缸的高度，对于猫来说，根本就是小菜一碟，所以她指定了一名卫兵。As a cat owner, Gran was no stranger to the athletic agility of a cat. The height of the vat could be cleared by a feline high jumper with ease and grace. So she appointed a guard. 奶奶给我布置任务的同时，那只猫就懒洋洋地躺在离水缸不远的地上，闭目养神。When this conversation was going on, the cat was not far from the vat, lounging on the floor with eyes closed.

奶奶打好酱油回到家,看到了这一幕: This is apparently what Gran saw when she came home with the soy sauce:

猫在原地未动,还是躺着,还在闭目养神。The cat had stayed put: still lying there enjoying a shut-eye. 我却成了一尊塑像,双肘撑着水缸盖,双手托着下巴,双眼紧盯着大碗里的鱼,一动不动! But what was I doing? I had turned into a statue, motionless, staring at the fish in the bowl, my chin propped in my palms and my elbows resting on the lid of the vat.

瞧,我奶奶没看错人,我就是一个忠于职守的卫兵! There you have it. I was as dutiful as a guard ought to be. Gran was a good judge of character.

虽然这件事我不记得了,但好几年后发生的另一个类似事件,我却记忆犹新。Although, as I said, I have no recollection of that incident, a similar case that took place many years later is still fresh in my memory.

那是在南京,我外公外婆家里。I was visiting my grandparents on my mother's side in Nanjing. 他们养了一只猫,还养了一些金鱼(对,又是一个猫和鱼的故事)。They had a cat, and some goldfish (oh yes, another cat-and-fish story). 隔三差五的,金鱼就会少一条,他们俩要是一起出门,家里没人的话,几乎每次都会发生金鱼失踪案。Every now and then they would lose a fish, particularly if they had both been out. 谁干的呢?头号嫌犯自然就是那只猫,破案线索并不复杂,不用请侦探、不用安装摄像头(那个时代也没有摄像头),也能推定。Did the cat nick them? My grandparents wouldn't put it past her. It wasn't a difficult whodunit to solve, even without Sherlock Holmes or a spy camera, which ordinary people didn't have at the time anyway. 只是证据缺失(等他们回家时,猫早已将现场清理完毕,从金鱼缸里溅出来的水也蒸发了,她在捞鱼时弄湿的手,也舔干了),又没有抓到现行,且不说金鱼忘性很大,即便幸存者记得是谁干的,也一定三缄其口,无法向主人指认凶手。It would have been an open-and-shut case had it not been for the fact that she was never caught red-handed (or wet-pawed) and by the time my grandparents got home, no conclusive evidence could be found, except for some faint dubious water stains, already dried, in the vicinity of the fish bowl. Positive ID from the surviving goldfish, famous for their three-second memory (though contradicted by modern research) and their conspiracy of silence? Fat chance. 因此只能严厉地质问她,是不是她干的,看她是否心虚,用眼神招供,然后施以某种惩罚(例如打屁股)。All my grandparents could do was subject her to the third degree and pin the crime on her, in the hope that her eyes would betray her by betraying her guilty conscience, at which point some form of penalty (such as corporal punishment zeroed in on her backside) could be meted out. 但猫的心理很强大,不像狗。狗知道自己做错了事,或者主人责怪它做错了事之后,最多掩饰一两秒,然后就撑不住了,低下头,既想琢磨主人的眼神,又不太敢看,只能满脑门皱纹地瞟主人两眼,用身体语言求饶:"我错了,对不起。您骂我吧,我该!不过,您要是饶了我呢……我就更爱您啦!"如果它做了一件事,但吃不准以人类的标准来看做得对不对,它会战战兢兢地看着主人的眼睛,摇着尾巴,抱着有罪推定的心理,等候你的发落。But cats are very good at hiding what is really going on in their heads, unlike dogs. When a dog knows or is told it has done something wrong, it might try to look innocent for a couple of seconds. But that's as far as its audacity would take them. Torn between the instinct to avert your lashing stare and the urge to find out what your eyes are saying, it would dip its head, steal a furtive glance at you (while wearing a guilt-racked look with a furrowed forehead) and tell you with its body language: 'It was my fault. I am sorry. If you tell me off, I deserve it. But if you spare me this time, I would love you even more!' If it has done something but is not sure if it is considered naughty or cute by human criteria, it would engage your eyes nervously and wag its tail with equal nervousness at the same time, trying to read your mind and second-guess your verdict while presuming itself guilty.

Leonoir and Gingerlet 伙伴行

话说南京外婆家每次发生了金鱼失踪事件后,脾气急躁的外公,懒得跟猫理论,只走上前二话不说揍她一顿,外婆连忙阻拦,让他别管。"猫不知道你为什么揍她,揍了也白揍。"外婆显然是护着猫的。Back to my grandparents' cat in Nanjing... Whenever a goldfish went missing, Grandpa, who had a much shorter fuse than Grandma, would propose a good thumping, to put her on the straight and narrow, without bothering with interrogation. Spank the fish-lifter but spare the inquisition, in other words. Grandma didn't want her cat to be hurt, so she would tell him to leave it to her. 'You cannot beat her up without telling her what the beating is for. If she doesn't know the reason, she would do it again regardless,' she would say in the suspect's defence. 外婆脾气很好,说话声音也很柔,她对这个小扒手说:"咪咪,我问你,你是不是调皮啦?吃了一条金鱼吧?你每天都有鱼吃,金鱼不是给你吃的。你这样就不乖了,我们不喜欢你了。"Grandma was a soft-spoken, mild-mannered lady. She would say to the pilferer, 'Meow Meow, let me ask you: Were you being naughty? Did you eat a goldfish? You have your own fish to eat every day. Goldfish are not for you. That's not being a good girl. We're going to stop liking you.' 猫懒洋洋地抬眼看看她,爱理不理、假装无辜地"喵"一声,意思是:"说什么哪?什么金鱼不金鱼的,我不知道!" The cat would cast a reluctant glance at her and favour her with a gruff, nonchalant 'meow' reply, meaning: 'What are you talking about? Goldfish? What goldfish?'

　　某个星期天,外公外婆要去拜访一位朋友,出门前关照我:"看好金鱼,别让猫得逞!" One Sunday, they were going to visit a friend. Before leaving, they asked me to make sure the cat wouldn't strike again. 他们一走就是四个小时,这期间我时而跟猫玩,时而观察金鱼,时而做做其他事情(例如研究怎样才能永久性地垫高某个桌腿,让桌子不再晃动)。They were gone for four hours, during which I alternated between playing with the cat, observing the goldfish and occupying myself with some other activities (like trying to work out a more permanent way of

- 47 -

keeping the dining table level）。外公外婆回家时，我正好处于"观察金鱼"的状态，也是纹丝不动，全神贯注地看着那几尾金鱼。When they came home, I happened to be in the 'observing the goldfish' mode, so they saw me planted in front of the fish bowl staring at the fish.

外公外婆之前已经听我母亲说过，我在崇明曾将"看(kān)鱼"任务当作"看(kàn)鱼"任务来执行，这回算是眼见为实了。他们一踏入家门，就发现我目光呆滞，盯着金鱼缸一动不动，立即联想到发生在崇明的那一幕，于是断定这四小时我一直处于观鱼状态！They had heard from my mother how I had interpreted the task of 'keeping an eye on the fish' as 'keeping my eyes on the fish' in Chongming. When they stepped through the door and saw me gazing at the fish in the bowl, they were reminded of the Chongming story and thought that I had been doing that nonstop for four hours.

他们问我时，我否认了，但否认得不是太坚决，以致他们以为我只是不好意思承认而已。从此，这个故事就成了家人和朋友津津乐道的长效笑料。I denied it when they asked me if I had been watching the fish（rather than watching over the fish）all that time, but my denial lacked firmness, giving them the impression that I was too embarrassed to admit it. From then on, this story joined the growing tally of amusing titbits about me and my idiosyncrasies bandied about among my family and their friends.

Leonoir and Gingerlet 伙 伴 行

拦路抢劫   The Catch Snatcher

我奶奶家的猫和外婆家的猫,虽然经常吃鱼,对不该吃的鱼也很感兴趣,偶尔甚至还偷吃,但他们没有他们的远方表亲小黄那样的机会,可以亲手捉鱼。The cats kept by my paternal and maternal grandmothers both had fish in their daily diet. They both showed a little bit too much interest in the fish they were not supposed to have and, when given half a chance, would not hesitate to pilfer the forbidden fish for their own consumption. But neither had the kind of opportunity their many-times-removed cousin Gingerlet had: to catch live fish with their own paws.

有一天,小黄叼着一条大小适中的鱼,匆匆回家,当时门敞开着,他不用爬窗户,就可以长驱直入。One day, Gingerlet rushed home with a moderately sized fish in his mouth. The door was open at that point, so he didn't have to get in through the window. 他照例进门后直奔厨房角落,打算在那里美美地吃上一顿生猛河鲜。He was following his established routine: The prey was to be spirited away to a corner of the kitchen where he could enjoy his fresh lunch in peace and quiet. 但我没放行,因为他进来后,我一眼就认出了,他嘴里叼着的正是一条非洲鲫鱼! But I didn't let him this time. I had recognised the fish in his mouth the very moment he stepped in: It was an 'African carp'.

非洲鲫鱼是俗称,学名是"莫桑比克罗非鱼"。African carp has a posh name: Mozambique tilapia (Latin: *Tilapia mossambica*). 兴化的非洲鲫鱼是我父亲引进的,因为非洲鲫鱼的众多优点中,有一个相当显著的特性,我记得很清楚,就是它能在水浅、低溶氧的水稻田里生存,而兴化是全国的产粮大县,主产水稻,养殖非洲鲫鱼既有地利优势,又能丰富当地的生态结构。My father was responsible for the introduction of Mozambique tilapia to Xinghua. This type of fish has a great many merits, but one of its best known characteristics, which I remember dis-

- 49 -

tinctly, is that it can survive and thrive in shallow waters like paddy fields, where the level of dissolved oxygen is low. Xinghua was one of the largest grain-producing counties in China and its number one crop was rice, so African carp was a perfect alien species to augment the county's biodiversity. 有一段时间，父亲全身心扑在非洲鲫鱼的繁殖上，每天都泡在鱼塘和养殖场，进行各种观察和实验，或者在家研究资料。我在寒暑假或周末，也会穿上防水服，陪他出入人工繁殖的车间，他边操作边向我讲解各个环节。For months and months on end, father devoted all his energies to the breeding of tilapia. He spent a lot of time observing and experimenting in the fish farm, around the fish ponds, or poring over the literature at home. During winter and summer holidays and on weekends, I would put on a waterproof wader and accompany him as he plied his craft in the breeding area and explained to me each and every step of the entire procedure. 这就是为什么我对非洲鲫鱼如此熟悉，不用靠近就能认出的原因。That's why I knew tilapia like the back of my hand and could instantly recognise one from a distance.

我突然冒出了一个念头。我知道非洲鲫鱼味道不错，好久没吃了，今天送上门来，这样的"礼物"我岂能拒绝？Suddenly, a thought flashed across my mind. I knew tilapia were tasty fish and I hadn't had any for quite some time. Now that one had been delivered to the door, literally, how could I say no to a 'gift' like this?

我让小黄停下。他听话地停下脚步，抬起头看着我，不知我想干什么。I told Gingerlet to stop, which he did. He looked up at me, wondering what I was going to do. 我走过去，蹲下来，用手拎着他的脖颈，喝令："张嘴！" I walked over, squatted down in front of him, grabbed him by the scruff of his neck and commanded: 'Open your mouth!' 他非但没有服从命令听指挥，反倒紧咬着鱼，紧闭着双眼，意思是："就不给你，你想怎样？"（不知为何，在我想象中，小黄的台词似乎带点台湾腔。）My order fell on deaf ears. The fish remained firmly clenched between his teeth. He closed his eyes, as if saying, 'Do as you wish, but I'm not going to let you have it.'

跟黑狮比，小黄算是非常听话的了，虽然在外捕鼠捉鱼，上天入地，骁勇善战，但在家对我们是百依百顺，被黑狮欺负了，也从不还击，不和家人发生正面冲突。用人类的概念来给他定性，他在外嫉恶如仇，在家高风亮节。Normally, Gingerlet was an obliging cat, more compliant than Leonoir. Though a highly decorated warrior that went on daily expeditions of conquest, ambushing his aquatic prey and battling the wicked rodents, Gingerlet was very submissive to his human 'superiors' at home and never ever gave us any trouble since he was a kitten. He was averse to confrontation with family members. As you read on, you'll find out that Gingerlet would not so much as strike back, as cats famously do, when he was bullied by Leonoir. In a nutshell, he was a magnanimous peace lover at home, quite the opposite of what he was like on his knightly escapades out there.

但这次，小主人要猫口拔鱼，这简直就是与虎谋皮嘛，他可不干了。这自然是情有可原的。But this time, when I asked him to surrender the spoil he had fought hard for, compliance was slow in coming, understandably. 看来君子动口不动手不管用了，动粗是不可避免的了。我把他的脑袋往后一拉，让他那湿漉漉的脸和嘴里衔着的那条非洲鲫鱼正对着我，然后我对他的鼻子"噗"地吹了一口气，这招很管用，他哆嗦了一下，一松嘴，鱼就啪地一声掉下来了。'Oh I see, gentlemanly negotiation is a little too tame for this, huh? A bit of manhandling is in order, I guess.' With that, I pulled his head back so I could look squarely at his wet face and the tilapia sandwiched in his mouth. I then blew at his nose. Puff! It worked. Reflex made him loosen his jaws and the fish plopped onto the floor.

他看了一眼瘫在地上奄奄一息的鱼，心里掂量了一下，寻思着从小主人手中夺回这条猎物的可能性微乎其微，不如送个顺水人情，于是走开了。He took one last look at the fish, now languishing on the floor. He weighed the odds. Realising it was well-nigh impossible to retrieve it from his young master anyway and that he would be better off giving it to him as a present (albeit an unintended one), he walked away.

我把自己用特制"气枪"明火执仗"拦路抢劫"得来的这条非洲鲫鱼交给母亲。她目睹了刚才那一幕，一边说"不得了了，这样的事你也做得出来？"一边笑着接过去，走进厨房，三下五除二就做出了一道鲜美无比的红烧鱼。我们吃之前，把鱼的头尾给了小黄，算是奖励他的"慷慨"进贡。I handed to my mother this tilapia that I had intercepted in my mugging heist with a special 'air gun'. She had watched the drama from the sidelines and the mischievous child in her found it rather amusing. While saying 'oh dear, how could you do that?' she took the fish, went into the kitchen and whipped up a scrumptious dish of braised tilapia. The head and tail of the fish were offered to Gingerlet as a reward for his 'generosity'.

这个故事，我曾经相当得意地对一些人说过，结果爱猫人士对我口诛笔伐，说我是假爱猫，真剥削，加之小黄年龄不大，我简直就是剥削童工，罪上加罪，跟招募、训练流浪儿的丐帮帮主有何区别？I related this story to various people before with an inappropriately proud tone of voice, only to draw a chorus of condemnation from cat lovers among them. They chastised me, calling me a fraud that pretended to love cats while harbouring an ulterior motive to exploit them. Even worse, Gingerlet being a young cat, exploitation of child labour became an aggravating circumstance that added to my culpability. Not to put too fine a point on it, I was not much better than Fagin, who made a business out of taking advantage of street urchins. 不过我充其量只是个偶犯，不是惯犯。当时我把此事想象成小黄给主人进贡，以示效忠，觉得蛮好玩的，但这毕竟违背了他的意愿，我心里多少有点过意不去。此后，小黄只需自给自足即可，无须为主人觅食了。I must add, in my own defence, that I was guilty only as a casual offender, not of recidivism. I had fantasised to my own amusement that the fish in question was a tribute payment from Gingerlet as a token of allegiance. However, I was also ashamedly aware of the strong-arm tactic I had employed. From then on, Gingerlet had all his catches to keep for himself and never had to go on a fishing trip on his master's account.

茅房纪实　Legend of Thatched Cottages

小黄在胁迫下给主人送过鱼,但黑狮从未奉献过任何食物。他当然不是小气鬼,只是他满腔热情献给我的、从外面搜刮来的"零食",都是脏兮兮的。唉,不说也罢。So, Gingerlet had to give up his fishy prey to me under duress on one occasion. Leonoir, on the other hand, never offered me anything humanly edible. He was an enthusiastic, generous giver all right, but whatever snacks he scavenged from outside were, to put it mildly, a bit lacking in the department of hygiene. Most of them were unmentionable. 但是我们屋后的某个角落里,也曾出过一个惊喜。可以说是天造之物吧? 就是在最不可能长出美食的地方,活生生冒出了个"宝贝"(简称"活宝")! One day, however, something edible sprang up from a certain nook and cranny behind our house. It was a serendipity, something weird and wonderful that appeared, as if by magic, in the most unlikely of places. 且容我慢慢道来。And thereby hangs a tale.

所谓"屋后的某个角落",就是一个"旱厕"。旱者,无水也;厕者,方便小屋也。无水,则无法顺顺溜溜地一冲了事;小屋,有点名不副实,因为"容器"往往很大。That most unlikely place was a latrine. Latrine is a WC, but without the W (so it's incapable of a royal flush); a toilet, but without the 'let' (it's usually a very large pit). "旱厕"已经算是文雅的叫法了,其实就是"茅房",说得更粗俗一点,就是"茅坑"、"粪坑"。It's a hole in the ground for the disposal of human waste. That's why it's also called a pit latrine. In Chinese, it's sometimes referred to, euphemistically, as 'thatched cottage' (because the pit is typically housed in a draughty makeshift structure with a possibly leaky thatched roof). Less idyllic than that is the alias of 'thatched pit' or, more explicitly (and rhymingly in English), 'shit pit'. I guess the English word 'bog' is as close to the imagery of a shit pit as it can get, and more graphic and phonetically apt...

如果你还没恶心得想吐，还扛得住的话，请允许我再描述一些细节，不是我对这种"下三路"的话题有着病态的兴趣，而是这种"基础设施"，现在不多见了，尤其在城市，所以我趁这个机会，用文字记录一下。If you are not the squeamish type and have not been totally repulsed by this topic so far, please allow me to fill you in on a little more details, not because I have a morbid lavatorial obsession or scatological fascination. No, not that. I simply don't want to miss this opportunity whereby I can record with words this type of 'infrastructure' that is increasingly rare in today's world, especially in urban settings.

通常，这样的茅坑，是在土坑里埋一口大缸（所以茅坑又叫"茅缸"或"粪缸"），缸口直径一两米，上面铺着两块平行的木板，起支撑人体

印有"世界厕所日"宣传口号的卫生纸。What better medium to carry the World Toilet Day publicity information?

的作用,这座"双木桥"中间的空隙就是通道,排泄物在地球引力的作用下,通过这个空隙,噗通或哗啦一声落入坑内。Typically, a shit pit is a tank buried in the ground (hence its other monikers 'thatched vat' and 'dump tank'). The opening of the pit, one or two yards across, is bridged with two parallel wooden planks to support the user. The gap that runs through this bridge over 'troubled water' provides passage for the discharged human waste free-falling into the receptacle, ending in a muffled plop or a messy splash.

旱厕除了不卫生之外,也有不少安全隐患,这大概是原始构造的"通病"。例如下雨天,"秋水龙吟"桥的木板很滑,稍不留神就惨了,落"汤"鸡的滋味可不好受。Pit latrines are rightly considered unhygienic and that's why there is a worldwide campaign to replace it with more modern alternatives. But that's not the only reason they are undesirable. The primitive structure is rife with safety hazards. For example, the bridge of sighs (and other noises) can get slippery on rainy days. You have to be extremely careful when you step on and off. A slip would land you in a fine 'pickle'.

有天我听到外面闹哄哄的,出去一看,原来是养殖场某个人家的孩子脚下一滑,掉进茅坑了。One day, there was a commotion outside our house. It turned out that a boy from the fish farm had slipped and fallen into the pit. 只见他在茅坑里几乎没顶,两手在空中乱抓,他的痛苦状,我就不细说了,暂且引用《呼兰河》里的一段描述,其余细节,请诸君发挥想象力脑补一下吧:"不料那马还是站不起来。马的脑袋露在泥浆的外边,两个耳朵哆嗦着,眼睛闭着,鼻子往外喷着秃秃的气。" When I saw him, he was all but in over his head, in that dire mire, his soiled hands grasping at the air. I shall refrain from depicting the sorry mess in graphic detail, assuming you can visualise it with the help of this excerpt from *Tales of Hulan River* by Hsiao Hung: 'In spite of that, the horse still couldn't stand up. Its head bobbing up from the mud, its ears quivering, its eyes closed, it was puffing through its nose in short, frantic

Leonoir and Gingerlet 伙伴行

spurts.' 不过男孩比萧红笔下的那匹马幸运,养殖场的大人很快就用船篙把他捞了上来。But that's not how the boy ended up, fortunately. A grown-up from the farm fetched a quant and fished him out promptly.

再说茅坑使用的姿势。使用者跨蹲在木板上,这种技巧,亚洲人好像生来就有,他们休息时就爱蹲着,十分钟甚至半小时,自然不在话下。So, what position do you assume when you go about your business in a pit latrine? The user steps onto the two planks, a foot on each, and squats down to do the necessary. Asian people seem to be born with this skill. They can sit on their haunches for 10 minutes or even half an hour with relative ease. After all, it's one of their resting positions. 但一些西方人,尤其是北欧人却觉得像我们这样下蹲或一直蹲着的姿势,很难。But the same cannot be said for some Westerners, especially those of Nordic descent, who find it very challenging to squat the way we do or to keep themselves in this position for anything longer than a few seconds. 例如,季麦天的舅舅尼尔森(有维京人血统),是一名英国军人,在阿富汗执行任务时,基本上都是在野地里"方便",他们的做法是拿一把铁锹,在地里挖个浅坑,事情办完了,就拿刚才挖出来的土盖上。咦,这方法是不是听起来很熟悉呢?我一直觉得,这简直就是从猫那里偷师学来的独门绝技!唉,算猫族倒霉,不去申请专利,瞧,被人盗用了吧? Take Nelson for example. Nelson is my son's maternal uncle. He is a British soldier of Viking stock. While on his tour of duty in Afghanistan, he and his mates used wilderness as public conveniences (very public and very convenient indeed) most of the time. This is how they did it: You take a shovel and dig a shallow hole in the ground. You deposit whatever you wish to deposit in there. When you are done, you cover it with the earth you have shovelled out earlier. Hang on... Does this procedure have a curiously familiar ring to it? Yes, I do think they plagiarised this proprietary but regrettably unpatented technique from feline inventors!

话说尼尔森每次挖完坑之后,怎么办事儿呢?如果是中国人,一定能轻轻松松蹲下去,高高兴兴站起来,期间可能还从容地抽支烟、哼支小曲儿什么的。So, when a hole was made in the ground, what would Nelson do next? A Chinese toilet goer would most probably go down on his haunches, nice and easy, and, after an indeterminate while, stand up again, light and happy. During that indeterminate while, he might enjoy a leisurely smoke or hum a cheery tune. 但尼尔森没那闲情逸致，因为他碰到了难题:蹲不下去！他其实是一名很健壮的军人，热爱运动，曾获军队轻量级拳击冠军(我跟他掰过手腕，虽然我在掰手腕方面有一定的实力，但他每次都是在半秒之内解决战斗，笑嘻嘻的眼神似乎在说："你怎么如此没有自知之明呢？")，他能扛着杠铃做深蹲动作，但身体结构决定了他难以维持标准的深蹲姿势，不是腿部无力承受，而是会失去平衡，人仰马翻！在这种地方人仰马翻，后果既可以想象又不堪设想。But Nelson didn't have that luxury. He faced a problem: He couldn't squat down just like that. Don't get me wrong, Nelson is a very strong, athletic soldier, a former lightweight boxing champion in his regiment. I had thought I was quite good at wrist wrestling, until I challenged him to a few bouts. He was always able to beat me in half a second while eyeing me quizzically: 'Where did you get the idea that you might stand a chance?' He could do barbell full squats, but his musculoskeletal structure is such that he is unable to keep his body in a heels-down squat for longer than a few seconds, not because his legs would give, but because he would lose balance and tip over backwards, a consequence that is, given the context, conceivably inconceivable.

因此，他只能把铁锹杵在坑旁，将锹柄把手顶在腋下，然后"拄"着铁锹，很不雅观地维持半蹲姿态，克服生理障碍，完成这个原本"不可能的任务"，夺取一场非军事胜利！He would plonk the shovel right next to the hole, place the D-shaped grip of the shovel handle under his arm, go into an undignified half squat and stay in that position while half hoisted on the shovel-turned-crutch. And that became his *modus operandi* for accomplishing a 'mission impossible', a pat solution to overcome his physical constraints and clinch a nonmilitary victory!

拳击冠军尼尔森。Nelson the champ, with a belt to prove it

Leonoir and Gingerlet 伙伴行

偶遇　An Encounter of Destiny

我跟父亲自然没有这样的身体结构性局限,"蹲坑"时从不觉得有什么技术障碍。It goes without saying that my father and I didn't have that handicap. As far as we were concerned, using pit latrines posed no technical or anatomical challenge whatsoever. 父亲更绝,在上厕所的时候,虽然不哼小曲儿(毕竟茅房里音效不佳),但会抽支烟,既"清新"空气,又促进思考。这是他说的。Father was no 'bathroom singer' (not least because the porous walls of the 'bathroom', if they existed at all, were an acoustic nightmare), but he would have a smoke while in the facility. According to him, it would serve as air freshener and help him think, killing two birds with one stone. 他很欣赏朱自清的散文《谈抽烟》,特别是文中这几句,说到他心坎儿上了:"再说那吐出的烟,袅袅地缭绕着,也够你一回两回地捉摸;它可以领你走到顶远的地方去。——即便在百忙当中,也可以让你轻松一忽儿。所以老于抽烟的人,一叼上烟,真能悠然遐想。他霎时间是个自由自在的身子,无论他是靠在沙发上的绅士,还是蹲在台阶上的瓦匠。有时候他还能够叼着烟和人说闲话;自然有些含含糊糊的,但是可喜的是那满不在乎的神气。这些大概也算是游戏三昧吧。"He was a fan of author ZHU Ziqing, whose works include a mildly provocative and supremely insightful little study on smoking. What my father could relate to the most in that mini classic is an observation that can be rudely (out of foolhardiness on my part) and crudely (not word for word) translated as follows: '*Moving on to the smoke that you puff out... it wafts and swirls, its elusiveness teasing a couple of attempts out of you to grasp it, visually and mentally; it transports you to the furthest place possible. It could always give you a respite, even when you were inundated with worldly chores. It is true, therefore, that an adept can drift into trance-like reverie with a cigarette*

- 59 -

between his lips. When that moment comes, he is free: It matters not if he is a gentleman lounging in an easy chair or a bricklayer sitting on his haunches on the doorstep. Lipping a cigarette doesn't stop him having a chitchat with another person, if he chooses to. Naturally he cannot help but slur and mumble a little, but an air of insouciance that comes with it is a welcome bonus. "Keenly mindful while wallowing in the unyoked humour of levity" - that would be an apt description, would it not?'

父亲永远在思考问题,这种时候也不例外。My father was always 'thinking'. There was no reason he should suspend his cerebral activity during his toilet visits.

有一天,他照常在屋后的茅房里一蹲三得:出恭、抽烟、思考。One day, he was going through his routine in that 'thatched cottage' behind our house, multitasking as usual: relieving himself, smoking and musing, all at once. 突然,他那沉思的目光,透过烟雾,被紧贴着缸边的一株小草拽了过去。Suddenly, a tiny plant caught his pensive eyes through the blue haze. It was clinging to the exterior of the pit. 他仔细一看,那小草是从缸和泥土之间的缝隙中钻出来的某种爬藤植物,叶子是这样的:He looked closer. It was some sort of climbing plant that had struggled through the interface between the vat and the surrounding soil.

也就是说,在那个历史瞬间,在地球上这个不起眼的茅房里,一个使用茅缸的家伙盯视着这株攀附茅缸的家伙,而后者同时也在盯视着我父亲,一个出于好奇,一个出于困惑。So, there was this moment in history when, inside an obscure primitive lavatory on the face of the earth, a toilet goer was peeping at a toilet creeper with idle curiosity while the latter was peering at the former with an equal measure of puzzlement. 好奇——我父亲想知道,长相如此陌生的植物到底是什么?困惑——那株植物在想,每天来上厕所的人不少,从来没人正眼看过我,今天这人哪根筋搭错了?My father was curious because he had never seen a plant with such leaves before and he wanted to identify it. The botanical stranger was puzzled because this man, out of so many people

Leonoir and Gingerlet 伙 伴 行

who had frequented this facility on a daily basis but had been completely oblivious to its existence, was showing a refreshingly intense interest in it.

父亲下意识觉得，这个小生命，非同寻常。回家后，很兴奋地告诉了我，然后带我回到茅房，再看个仔细。Father's instinct jolted him into the realisation that this was no average climber. He came home and excitedly shared his discovery with me. He then took me back to the loo for a closer examination.

只见那株稚嫩的蔓藤，翠绿色的，长约20多厘米，沿缸攀缘，它的两旁是粪缸的褐色和泥土的黑色，我似乎能在绿头苍蝇飞舞的嗡嗡声和茅坑特有的浓重的气味中，嗅到它吐露的清香。There it was, before my eyes - a quivering tender vine, dripping in a green as tender. It was about seven or eight inches long, clinging to and extending along the wall of the vat, its verdure sandwiched between the earthen brown of the vat and the earthen black of the soil. Maybe it was just my imagination, but it was breathing out a cool, fresh scent, reaching my nose through a thick, putrid miasma of toilet odour, stirred into wafts of varied intensity by a swarm of bluebottles that were humming and bumbling around.

西瓜叶。(来源:维基百科)*A Watermelon vine.(© wikipedia)*

父亲用带着三泰腔的崇明话说:"我分析过,可能有人蹲了格垯咯时候勒嗨吃瓜(亏他想得出),瓜子就吐在了面前,其中有一粒瓜子长成了格个瓜秧。最有可能的就是西瓜。不过我唔没仔细看过西瓜格瓜秧,唔没把握。"Father said, in his Chongming dialect laced with a hint of the local accent, 'I thought about it. It looks as though someone was eating a melon while going toilet (a cringeworthy thought) and spat the seeds round him. One of the seeds has grown into this seedling. The most likely fruit is watermelon, but I'm not sure as I have never carefully studied watermelon vines.' 我听了很兴奋:"会长出西瓜来伐?"父亲说,很有可能,不过还得问问别人才能确认,但同时还得保密,否则捣蛋鬼可能会把它弄坏。His analysis thrilled me. I asked, 'So there will be an actual watermelon growing out of this?' Father confirmed that it was highly probable. He added that he needed to consult someone more knowledgeable, just to be certain, and make sure at the same time that the existence of this scrambler remained a secret, lest some wayward kid mess about and kill it.

此后几天,我每天都去茅房,就是为了给瓜秧浇水,观察瓜秧的长势。我小心翼翼地用碎砖和树叶筑成一个保护它的"掩体",并根据需要不时调节这个掩体的朝向和结构。这个掩体必须满足三个条件:(1)让蹲茅坑的人从蹲位上无法直接看到瓜秧;(2)不影响日照;(3)看不出是刻意堆砌,让人产生怀疑的"建筑物"。In the days that followed, visiting the loo for this unconventional purpose became a daily routine for me. I would water the plant and check out how it was doing. I built a shelter for it with meticulous attention, using bits of brick and tree leaves. I adjusted the orientation and structure of the shelter as and when I deemed it necessary. The shelter had to satisfy three conditions: (1) that it must so shield the plant as to obstruct the line of sight of a toilet 'squatter'; (2) that it would not block the sun out; and (3) that it would not look like a fishy 'purpose-built' structure.

有一天,父亲的一位同事顺道来我家取一件工具,他告别时,父亲假装不经意地问了一句:"哦,问一下,西瓜叶子是什么样子的?" One day, a colleague of my father's swung by our house to pick up a tool. When he was leaving, my father asked him a question, with studied casualness to mask its specificity, 'Oh, by the way, do you happen to know what watermelon leaves look like?'

那人的答案完全出乎我们的意料。他不假思索地答道:"西瓜叶子啊? 你家后头屎缸旁边的那根藤,就是西瓜藤。" The answer took us completely by surprise. Without even pausing to think, the guest replied, 'Watermelon leaves? Oh, you know the vine next to the crap hole behind your house? That's a watermelon plant.'

我看到父亲身体僵住了,他瞟了我一眼,只是"哦哦"了两声,什么也没说。送走那人后,他回到家里,我们四目对视,突然同时爆发出大笑……父子俩笑啊笑啊,把肚子都笑疼了。Father froze. I saw that. He shot a secret glance at me. He didn't say anything other than acknowledging the reply with some inscrutable noises. He saw the guest off and came home. We looked at each other. Then, suddenly and simultaneously, father and son cracked up. We were all but 'rofl'. I laughed so hard I had a stitch in my side.

在我的悉心照护下,"出污泥而不染"的西瓜藤茁壮成长,但由于我是第一次当瓜农,在它生长的某些环节,可能措施不当,也可能它所处的环境毕竟比较恶劣/心,它实在没办法总是强迫自己"开心",最后结出的瓜,虽然让我激动不已,越看越喜欢,但并没有越长越大。I can pride myself on the fact that the watermelon plant continued to thrive thereafter, cutting a pristine, unsoiled figure as it rose from the 'soil', a credit to the foul but fertile. However, although the actual fruit was a constant source of joy for me and this joy was growing by the day, the melon did not grow in tandem with my delight and its size remained stunted after a certain point. It is possible that I, an inexperienced orchardman, was guilty of inaction when certain action was called for or had applied the wrong interventions at the wrong time. Maybe it was simply down to the unfortunate fact that it had to call an inclement facility home, where it couldn't possibly keep smiling all the time.

"污瓜". The overnourished melon.

Leonoir and Gingerlet 伙伴行

收获　**The Harvest**

秋天很快就到了。那时候的四季比现在分明,换季相当准时,一阵秋风吹过,暴露在外的皮肤就会起鸡皮疙瘩,哪怕阳光依然热辣,但风里透出的那丝飕飕的凉意,谁都能感受到。It wasn't long before autumn arrived. In those days, seasonal variations were distinct and seasonal changes punctual. An autumn blast would leave your exposed skin tingling with goosebumps. The sun might still be beating down with considerable intensity, but it was impossible to miss the presentiment of chill in the wind.

眼看西瓜藤开始枯黄,那只"独生"的西瓜仔也无望长得更大了,父母劝我把它摘下来,否则会烂在"地里"。The watermelon vine began to turn brown. The lone dwarf of a melon seemed to have made up its mind not to grow any bigger. My parents advised me to harvest it. Otherwise it might rot away 'in the field', they warned. 我有点舍不得,这出西瓜生命剧这么快就进入尾声了,但他们说的确实有道理。于是我到茅房小心翼翼地将这只小西瓜从藤上摘下,在手里掂了掂,我爱吃西瓜,有鉴别力,可以准确判断一只瓜熟没熟、甜不甜,这只瓜显然没有熟透,估计也不会太甜,但也没辙了。Sad as it was that this motivational saga about an odds-defying watermelon was coming to its finale so soon, I had to accept my parents' advice. I went to the thatched closet and gingerly pulled the Lilliputian melon off its vine. I held it with both my hands to give it a feel. I was a watermelon connoisseur. I could tell with unfailing accuracy whether a watermelon had ripened and whether it was sweet enough. Obviously, this diminutive fruit in my hands was neither sufficiently ripe nor sufficiently sweet. But there was nothing I could do about it. 我就带着遗憾和期盼交织的心情,捧回家交给了母亲。I went home and handed it over to my mother. I wished it could have grown to a 'normal' size. I wished it could have kept on growing, forever. I wished... But at the same time, I was also curious: What would it taste like?

　　我们吃这只瓜的时候，似乎在举行一种庄严的"仪式"。There was something ceremonial about the way we consumed the watermelon. 先是由母亲翻来覆去又洗又刷，她有洁癖，特别注重这个环节，非亲自动手不可。The 'ceremony' began with my mother, a stickler for hygiene, scrubbing and washing the melon over and over again, which she considered to be of paramount importance. It was so important that she had to do it herself. 接着父亲把砧板洗净，擦干，再把西瓜放在上面，我和母亲在一旁"围观"。Then my father took over. He cleaned the chopping block and placed the melon on it. Mother and I stood on either side of the table to watch the action. 父亲手起刀落，西瓜应声而开，我们眼前看到的是色泽和质感"正常"的瓜瓤和黑色的瓜子！Father's cleaver fell and slashed the melon in half. What we saw was normal-looking pulp of normal texture, pink, studded with black seeds. 我激动得心都快跳出来了！I was so excited my heart very nearly popped out of my chest! 父亲补了两刀，切成了四块，我急不可耐地拿起一块，张大嘴，"夸嚓"一口咬了下去，然后如释重负般地感慨了一句"名言"："污瓜哪能呒没污格味道啊？" Father then quartered the melon. Impatiently, I grabbed a piece and took one huge, juice-splashing bite... before blurting out an exclamation of relief and elation. It was a rhetorical question that later became a source of amusement for my family and relatives: 'How come a shit melon doesn't taste like shit?'

Leonoir and Gingerlet 伙伴行

偶像小鹤　My Childhood Best Friend

　　这本书原本是说动物的，结果却花了不少篇幅介绍一只西瓜，而西瓜是植物。但这个故事太好玩了，我怎能不说呢？This book is supposed to be all about animals, but I ended up spending ages and pages waffling on about a particular watermelon, and watermelons are plants. I hope I could be forgiven for the digression by virtue of the fact that the story was too wickedly funny not to share with my son and my other readers.

　　如果要说植物的故事，我得另外写一本书，专门说说我的植物朋友，这里就"简短"地再说一个关于树的故事。I would have to write a separate book on my plant friends, if I were to go into any detail. But while I am at it, please allow me to say 'a few' words about a certain tree here. 在我的植物朋友中，最重要的是一棵香椿树和一棵榆树。The most important of my botanical buddies were a toon tree and an elm. (By the way, the toon tree has an honorific designation: *Toona sinensis*, which means Chinese toon). Toon sounds like a cousin of cartoon, but they have no connection whatsoever and neither does any justice to the other. So I prefer to call it by its Chinese name Xiangchun, which has a nice ring to it as well as a very auspicious connotation: a fragrant tree of eternal spring, a symbol of longevity!

　　先说那棵榆树吧，它命苦、命短，一大群可恶的虫子把它的叶子吃光后，它就一命呜呼了。But longevity, alas, is what its friend, the poor little elm, didn't have. It died after its leaves were set upon and ravaged by a horde of dastardly insects. 它来到我家，纯属偶然。缘于学校组织的一次植树造林活动。每名学生必须先买好一株树苗，在活动的当天，集体到郊外植树。我事先用五分钱买了一株榆树苗，靠墙放着，但活动那天我重感冒，没法参加，只好把树苗种在自家院子里了。It was by accident that the elm joined our family. My school had organised a tree-planting event. Each pupil was asked to buy a sapling. We would then go to a designated place in the suburbs and plant our trees there. I had shelled out five cents for a young elm, but I was taken ill with a bad cold on the day of the event. So the tree ended up in our yard, not in the suburbs.

但那棵香椿树就完全不同了，它显然比榆树聪明，是树中佼佼者。虽然也遭到了大规模的害虫袭击，但它并没有坐以待毙，反倒使了个绝招。The Xiangchun tree was a different case. In terms of intelligence, it was a cut above the rest, or above the elm at least. When overrun with pests, it didn't act like a sitting duck resigned to its fate. It fought back, in a clever way...

我们家搬到北郊的水产养殖场后，我也给那棵香椿树搬了家。After we had moved from our old house to the fish farm, which was located to the north of the town (for better air, more space and proximity to where my father was working), I started a project to relocate the Xiangchun. 跟我一起完成这项移植工程的，是我的邻居，是我童年时代最要好的一位小伙伴——小鹤（吴元鹤），也是当年让我仰视的两个偶像之一（另外一位是我父亲）。Help came in the form of Xiao He ('Little Crane'), whose full name is WU Yuanhe. He was my neighbour and one of my best childhood friends. He was also the byword for whiz-kid in my dictionary. (The other person I idolised was my father.)

小鹤比我大三岁，因顽皮著称，在校学习成绩不好，有时还逃学，上课迟到时，为了掩饰自己的尴尬、"活跃"课堂气氛，他会同手同脚迈着正步走进课堂，同学们见了哄堂大笑。课堂气氛是活跃了，但少不了挨老师加倍责骂。Xiao He, three years my senior, was known in the neighbourhood as the naughty one. His school took a dim view of him for his poor academic results, for his chronic truancy and for marching into the classroom in side-to-side goose-step when he was late for class. 'To ease my embarrassment and lighten the mood,' he explained, in defence

Leonoir and Gingerlet 伙伴行

of his clownish walk. Lighten the mood he did, as his classmates would fall about giggling at his antics. But the teacher's strictures coming his way also redoubled. 当时"机器人"这个概念在中国还没有普及，想必他现在已经意识到了，早在四十年前他就走出了机器人的经典步态！In those days, robots were unheard of in China. I'm pretty sure he is aware by now that he was aping the classic robot walk four decades ago without even realising it. 但他创造力很强，心灵手巧，富于幽默感，有着天然的审美能力，在我心目中是集发明家、工程师、艺匠于一身的神奇叛逆少年！哦，差点忘了，他歌也唱得很好。我母亲是南京师范学院音乐系毕业的，她从专业的角度，对小鹤的嗓音"本钱"赞不绝口。But that did not take away from the fact that he was quick-witted, very good with his hands, highly creative, humorous and blessed with natural aesthetic acumen. I looked up to him as a remarkable rebel, a gifted maverick, an impish embodiment of inventor, engineer and craftsman all rolled into one. But that's not all. He also had a terrific tenor voice, a lump of coal with diamond potential, according to my mother, who is a musician by training. 他能用一截树木、一把刀，在没有图纸的情况下，完全凭自己的想象力和对流体力学的基本理解，雕刻出一艘精美的快艇模型，里面装上一只小马达、两节一号电池，连上他自制的水面传动系统和螺旋桨，再经过几次水上试验、船体精整、叶片微调，快艇就能在鱼塘里劈波斩浪了。Without the benefit of any technical drawings whatsoever, he was able to craft a stunning model speedboat with a block of wood, a knife and nothing else. It was based on a design concept conjured up by him with the help of a fertile imagination and a rudimentary knowledge of hydrodynamics. He would put in a small electric motor and a couple of D-size batteries and connect the motor to a watertight power train and a screw propeller, both hand-made by himself. After a couple of break-ins followed by fine-tuning of the boat's contour and adjustment of the propeller blades, the boat would come alive, tearing along in one of the fish ponds. 后来他嫌船速不够快，把第一艘快艇送给了我，自己又造了一

台迷你柴油蒸汽机,为他的新船提供大马力动力。But he found that the boat's velocity left a lot to be desired. What he wanted was something more exciting, so he gave his first motorboat to me as a present and went on to build a diesel-powered steam engine to provide greater thrust for his next cutter.

言归正传。小鹤告诉我,下雨天不能给树挪窝儿,所以我们等到天空放晴了,才给它搬家。Anyway, back to tree relocation. Xiao He told me that one shouldn't replant a tree when it's raining, so we waited till the sun came out. 我们一人一把锹,合力在树周围挖了一个大坑,把香椿树连根拔起。We each had a shovel to work with. We dug a large and reasonably deep crater round the base of the tree, so the Xiangchun could be yanked out of its residence, along with its roots that were held together by clods of soil.

从旧家到新家,步行大概要三十分钟,我就扛着这棵跟我一样细细长长,一摇三晃的香椿树上路了,小鹤提着一把锹,殿后。The new house was half an hour's walk from our old home. I put the wiry Xiangchun on my shoulder (forming a cross with my lanky body) and set off. Xiao He brought up the rear with a shovel in his hand. 树的根部像我的脑袋一样,挺大的一坨,根须黑乎乎乱蓬蓬的,像我的头发,根部冲前,树梢在我身后。这幅图景够滑稽了吧?Picture this, if you will: I had a disproportionately large head atop of my flagpole of a body and this tree also sported a huge root clump, as dark and messy as my hair. The tree rested on my shoulder with its roots facing forwards and the treetop pointing backwards. Oh, charming! 当时是初春,它过冬时把去年的枝叶全割舍了(不知所有香椿树是否都这样,还是说我的这棵与众不同),今年还没开始冒芽,所以树梢光秃秃的,看上去只是树干的一部分,只是比其他地方更脆弱而已。The treetop had nothing on it, no leaves nor branches. It was just the top part of the trunk, a more vulnerable part, that is. It was early spring. New leaves had yet to return to the tree that had shed all its foliage (and all its branches) before last winter. To this day, I still don't know if this branch-shedding behaviour along with pre-winter defoliation was unique to my tree or common to this species.

最后一段路，是我们新家鱼塘边的那条泥路，之前曾经描述过。当时黑狮还没来我家，所以那一天没有动物来迎接我们，只有一头水牛驮着一个放牛娃，从我们旁边慢悠悠地走过。在最后一个拐角处，迎面走来了一个男人，他从我旁边擦身而过的瞬间，我正好拐弯，我忘了身后还有一长截树，没有调整方向，树梢一下子打到了那人的脑袋！正是一次不幸的"歪打正着"。The last leg of our journey was along a dirt path by the fish ponds, which I have described before. I had not adopted Leonoir at the time, so there was no animal to greet us on that road, except for a buffalo, who strolled past us at sloth speed carrying its young tender on its back. At the last bend, we saw a man walking towards us. He was passing us by just as I was turning into the other road. I had forgotten I had a long stick of a tree on my shoulder and the bulk of it was behind me, so I hadn't taken any precaution... 'Whack!' The tree-top hit his head. It was an unintended bullseye! 我听到身后传来"啊"的一声，自己脑袋里马上"嗡"的一声，知道不好了。一扭头，看见一张气急败坏、涨得通红的脸。那张因恼火而扭曲的脸突然开始咆哮："你谨啊说，你谨啊说？" I heard a loud 'ouch' from behind, echoed by an equally loud 'boom' inside my head: I knew in that instant what I had done. I turned round and saw an ogre's face, livid with rage. That face, gnarled by exploding fury, broke into a snarl: 'What do you say? What do you say?' 我吓懵了，脑子里一片空白，在那个瞬间根本听不懂他的问题到底是什么意思，更不知道如何回答。Petrified and nonplussed, my mind went blank. 'What's the right answer to his question?' was all I could think of. In fact, I wasn't even sure that I knew what he meant by that question. 就在我张口结舌的当儿，那人一把抓住香椿树梢，一边恶狠狠地盯着我，一边开始扳树梢，但扳树是慢动作，看得出他只是在威胁，逼我作出反应。For a moment, I was too overwhelmed to react, verbally or otherwise. The man grabbed ahold of the tip of the tree and started bending it as he was shooting a menacing stare at me. I could tell, though, that he was only threatening to snap the treetop off in order to force a response out of me, because he was doing it in slow motion. 就在香椿树生死存亡的那一刻，小鹤一个箭步跃到那人面前，两手紧紧握住他那只扳树梢的手，让他停下，同时像连珠炮一样说了一串"对不起"："对不起，对不起，对不起，叔叔！不是故意的，不小心，对不起，对不起，对不起……" At that precise juncture, when the life of my Xiangchun was hanging by a thread, Xiao He lunged at that man like a flash. He held his wrists in a firm lock, so he couldn't bend it any further, while showering him with a slew of rapid-fire apologies: 'Sorry, sorry, sorry, sorry... Uncle, sorry, he didn't mean it. Just being careless. Sorry, sorry, sorry...'

我缓过神来，也马上对他连连道歉。现在想想，那人其实心地还是蛮善良的，因为我们一服软，他马上就松手，放过了我，也放过了香椿树。I woke up from my catatonic stupor and started apologising to him, too. And profusely. When I play back that episode in my head now, I can see that the enraged victim of my blunder was actually rather forgiving, because as soon as we said sorry, he let go of the tree and spared me any further reprimand. 他哼了一声，走了。我看着他的背影，发现他没有用手去揉脑袋，估计没大碍，心里稍稍好受一些。He left us in a huff. I watched him walking away and noticed that he did not rub any part of his head. So, no damage done, I thought to myself. It eased my guilty conscience a little. 小鹤问我："你刚才怎么傻啦？为什么不道歉呢？"我答道："我彻底吓懵了，话都说不出来，而且也不知道他的问题怎么回答。"小鹤说："你不管他说什么，马上道歉，而且要低声下气连连道歉，'礼多人不怪'，这样人家的气才能消掉，大人嘛，容易来火，我们多赔点小心没坏处。多悬啊？辛辛苦苦扛来的树，差点就报销了！" Xiao He asked me, 'What happened to you just now? You didn't say or do anything. Why didn't you apologise?' I said, 'I was scared witless and shitless. I couldn't get a word out of my mouth. And I didn't know how to answer his question.' Xiao He said, 'You don't worry about what the other person says. You just apologise, okay? Right away. And help yourself to a *massive* slice of humble pie. Flattery will get you everywhere and so will apology, you know. That's how you appease your victim. It wouldn't hurt to keep your wits about you when you deal with prickly grown-ups. That was such a close shave. It took us so much trouble to get the tree over here and he nearly killed it!'

他见我不做声了，从我肩上接过有点蔫耷耷的香椿树，自己扛着，在前头走了，还吹起了口哨，吹的是《扬鞭催马送公粮》之类的旋律。
Still reeling from the shock, I fell silent. He took over the tree, now looking a little the worse for wear, put it on his shoulder and walked on in front of me. He started whistling, too. What was the tune he was whistling? I don't remember now, but it could be that seemingly ubiquitous flute number, 'Whips Crack, Horses Gallop, to the Socialist Commune We Deliver Our Harvest'.

香椿的口福　A Boon to the Toon

到了新家屋后的空地，我跟小鹤都特别开心，因为香椿树劫后余生，即将搬入它的"新居"了。Xiao He and I were in a triumphant mood when we got to the open field behind my new home: My precious Xiangchun, having survived a life-threatening crisis, was about to move into its new 'abode'.

小鹤眯眼看了看前面的房子和四周，估算了一下这棵树每天可以晒到多长时间的阳光，以及四季变化对日光浴时间的影响，然后用脚尖指着某个地方，说："就这里吧！"我们就开始轮流操锹挖起坑来。Through squinted eyes, Xiao He surveyed the house in front as well as the surroundings, to gauge the amount of sunlight the tree would get each day and how the seasonal change would impact its daily sunbathing time. He then pointed at a spot with his foot and said, 'This is it.' With that, we started digging, taking turns to use the only shovel we had. 坑挖好后，他提议："来，我们往坑里撒泡尿，算是给它庆贺乔迁之喜。"When the hole was ready, he proposed we each spend a penny to give the tree a house-warming gift. 但我记得《十万个为什么》说过，新鲜尿液不能用作肥料，在发酵过程中会把植物"烧"死的。于是，我弱弱地表达了我的疑问。I apologetically challenged his proposal because I remembered I had read in *Hundred Thousand Whys* (arguably China's most popular encyclopaedic science primer series, modelled on and inspired by Russian writer Ilya Marshak's seminal work by the same hyperbolic title) that fresh urine is caustic and the fermentation process may kill, rather than fertilise, plants. 小鹤胸有成竹地说："我知道，没得事。小便发酵快，渗到泥里，很快就发酵了，就可以做肥料了。我们尿完，等下子，再把树栽下去。" Xiao He was undeterred by my scepticism. He sounded a hundred percent sure about what he was doing: 'I know that, but it's okay.

Leonoir and Gingerlet 伙伴行

Urine decays really fast. Once in the soil, the fermentation is complete before you know it and we'll have a very good fertiliser. We can wait a little before putting the tree down though.' 我崇拜小鹤，对他自然言听计从，再加上他这么一解释，我疑虑顿消，痛痛快快地跟他一起，将液体肥料浇洒到土坑里。I had put Xiao He on a pedestal and whatever he said carried a lot of weight. His explanation threw my doubts straight out of the window. So, there we were, the two of us, sprinkling the liquid fertiliser (or its precursor) into the pit with blithe abandon.

我们很快完成了尿液的露天垂直输送。当时我开始想象琥珀色的液体如何慢慢渗入褐色的泥土，如何经过化学变化，化为香椿树可口的营养品。Before long, we completed the vertical delivery of urine in the open. I began visualising how the amber liquid was slowly seeping into the brown soil and how it was going through a chemical process and becoming delectable nutriments for my Xiangchun.

在我遐想时，在等候尿液从复杂化合物分解为简单化合物的过程中，小鹤又在忙什么呢？While I was picturing that scenario in my mind, while we were waiting for the urine to break down into simpler chemicals, what was Xiao

小鹤和我，正在施肥。*Xiao He and me, feeding the tree.*

He doing? 他在找东西。他环顾四周,看到不远处的地上躺着一滩已经晒干的人粪,喜出望外,怪叫一声宋江的口头禅"正合吾意"(我们俩当时正在如饥似渴地看《水浒传》),立即操起铁锹,直奔过去。He was scanning the lie of the land, searching for something. Then, he spotted, not far from us, a cake of sun-dried human excrement lying shapelessly on the ground. He yodelled 'Suits me' (the literal, expanded translation of his original words being 'this is a perfect fit for my intent', roughly equivalent to 'oh, goodie' or 'just what the doctor ordered' in the vernacular of a less formal register; used to excess by SONG Jiang, the artful ringleader of a rebel group featured in the classic novel *Water Margin*, whose enraptured readership included both of us at the time), picked up the shovel and made a beeline for it. 还没等我缓过神来,他已经铲起那泡屎,走回树坑,手腕一抖,那饼固体肥料就啪的一声,不偏不倚地落在了坑底。Before I realised what was going on, he scooped up the poop, walked back to the pit and, with a flick of the wrists, sent the payload to the bottom of the tree's new home in one clean move. 他得意地扭头对我说:"这泡屎在这块已经很多天了,早就发酵了,营养丰富啊!香椿树很有口福!" Visibly pleased with himself, Xiao He turned round and said to me, 'This turd is a godsend. It has been lying around for days, so it's fully fermented by now. What a lucky tree! Now it has a nutritious kick-start in waiting!' 要是放在今天,我俩肯定会击掌,只是当年击掌动作还没发明出来呢,古人的额手相庆,我们又学不来。A high-five would have suited the occasion, but this celebratory gesture hadn't been invented yet, let alone introduced into China.

　　就这样,我的香椿树有惊无险、坐北朝南,在用沤肥浸润的新落脚点安家落户了。That's how my Xiangchun was uprooted from its old home, had a scary brush with death on the way and resettled in a new south-facing, crap-padded crash pad that was made more welcoming with the help of some warm organic liquid compost.

Leonoir and Gingerlet   伙伴行

智胜   A Battle of Wits

前面说到，那棵短命的榆树是因为叶子被虫子蚕食得千疮百孔而夭折的，而那种虫害，香椿树也未能幸免。Earlier I mentioned briefly a short-lived elm that succumbed to the onslaughts of swarms of borers. It did not recover from the trauma that its bug-riddled foliage had sustained. Unfortunately, the same infestation also descended upon the Xiangchun. 但香椿树坚韧不拔，不畏强暴，跟虫子斗智斗勇，最后打败了它的天敌。But Xiangchun was a survivor and a very resilient, resourceful fighter. That battle, thank goodness, ended in the tree's victory.

当我第一次看到香椿叶子上爬满了小虫子时，心里拔凉拔凉的，知道不妙了。When I first saw tiny insects crawling on the Xiangchun's leaves, a chill crawled down my spine. My heart sank. 当时我家没有、也无法获得农药，来杀灭这些虫子，我只能每天提一桶水，到屋后，往树上洒水，然后摇树干，希望把虫子淹死或吓跑，但又不敢摇得太使劲，得悠着点儿，怕伤着树。We had no pesticide at home, nor did we have access to any, so I couldn't kill those pests with poison. All I could do was take a bucket of water round the back of the house each day, sprinkle water on the tree and then shake its trunk, hoping to drown the vermin or at least put them off by making their life very uncomfortable. But I had to hold myself back and tried not to shake the tree too hard lest I end up hurting, not helping, it.

我凭空想出来的这些招数毫无科学依据，《十万个为什么》里面的"为什么"再多，也不可能有治虫良方。My tricks didn't do the trick: I had conceived them out of thin air; science didn't come into the equation at all; and the impressively named know-it-all book, *Hundred Thousand Whys*, didn't ask nor answer enough whys after all. 只见香椿的状态每况愈下，树叶被虫子啃出了密密麻麻的窟窿，我眼睁睁看着它们枯萎，心

- 77 -

疼死了，却束手无策，只能干着急。The condition of the Xiangchun steadily deteriorated. Its holey leaves withered, right before my eyes. My heart was bleeding. I had to let it bleed because there was nothing I could do. 有一天，我突然发现，情况更糟了，连树枝都开始蔫巴了。As if that wasn't bad enough, the branches started to wilt too, I sadly noticed one day. 最后，我的香椿树变成了一根无叶、无枝的"光棍"，它那颀长的树干，茕茕然杵在屋后的空地上。生命的凋零跟暮春的暖风，构成了鲜明的反差。What was left of the Xiangchun in the end was a *guanggun*, a 'naked rod' (but longer and more slender than the sesame-less breakfast doughnut), defoliated and debranched, cutting a lonesome, lanky figure in the open grounds behind our house, a stark contrast to the balmy zephyrs of late spring. 不过，在叶落枝折的过程中，我注意到了一个奇异的现象：有些树叶没有被蚕食，完好无损、绿得发亮，却"主动"飘落；有些树枝明明长得好好的，一夜之间却"主动"枯萎，掉在树根四周。But before it got to this stage, when it was shedding leaves and branches, I noticed something extraordinary was going on. Some of the leaves and branches had not fallen victim to the entomological warfare. They were unscathed and thriving with radiant verdure, and yet they were coming off the tree for no apparent reason, carpeting the area round its root. Sometimes this would happen overnight. The whole process seemed deliberate and *proactive* on the part of the tree. 虽然香椿树这种行为似乎展现了一种大义凛然、玉石俱焚的英雄气概，但我脑袋里还是画了一个大大的问号。This behaviour could be interpreted as a laudable death-defying act of heroism, of uncommon courage to embrace its ruination as well as that of its archenemy. But that turn of events was a mystery nonetheless.

一个月之后，谜底揭晓了。The explanation for the anomaly surfaced a month later. 我的香椿树以令人惊诧的速度，长出了新枝、新叶，我这才恍然大悟……It dawned on me when the Xiangchun's new branches and leaves began to shoot at a jaw-dropping speed. 原来，香椿

Leonoir and Gingerlet 伙 伴 行

树认识到,自己是一棵无法逃跑、无法主动还击的乔木,遭到虫子的袭击,只能以静制动、以逸待劳。It transpired that the Xiangchun had realised - and accepted - the fact that the only response that a tree like itself could give to an assault by animals, which by definition are mobile organisms, was to leverage its stationary position, as well as the patience that came with it, to sit out its nemeses, since neither fight nor flight was an option. 但是,如果任由这些害虫肆无忌惮地啃噬,它也会性命不保的,所以一味被动忍让也不行,还得想办法以某种形式抵抗一番。But complete inaction or a grin-and-bear-it attitude was not an option either because, given half a chance, the pests would nibble, gnaw, chomp and devour their way to the demise of the tree. It had to put up some semblance of resistance, one way or another. 香椿的嫩叶,又叫香椿头,是美食家钟爱的食材,可口无毒,营养丰富,适合凉拌,香椿树不可能改变自己的属性,怀着恶毒之心,连夜赶工制造出毒汁,把这些虫子置于死地而后生。The budding leaves of Xiangchun, also known as toona spears, are the love of foodies in China. They are nutritious, nontoxic and full-flavoured, perfect as salad greens. Obviously, the Xiangchun was not equipped to change its basic attributes all of a sudden, start producing vengeful venom and survive its tormentors by poisoning them to death.

那么怎么办呢?在这生死存亡的关头,香椿树将《三十六计》中的"假痴不癫"计、"李代桃僵"计、"釜底抽薪"计和"金蝉脱壳"计进行优化组合,发明了一种独门绝技,以守为攻阻击外侮,以魔法驱魔虫,实现咸鱼大翻身!Was there a way out? At this juncture of life and death, the Xiangchun worked out a very cunning plan, possibly by drawing inspiration from four of the *Thirty-Six Stratagems*(of ancient Chinese warcraft), namely, the trick of feigned insanity(to encourage the enemy to drop their guard), the trick of sacrificing a plum tree to save a peach tree(to pull the wool over the enemy's eyes), the trick of removing firewood from under the cauldron(to deprive the enemy of their essential resources)and the trick of slinking away like a cicada shedding its shell(to give the enemy a golden handshake in the form of a dispensable part of itself). With this cunning plan, the Xiangchun successfully repelled the bug invasion with a defensive strategy and exorcised the leaf snatchers with its shapeshifting magic. It was reborn, like a breakfast kipper coming back to life. "皮之不存,毛将焉附?"果然,那些害虫跟树枝树叶一同坠地后,随着食物的枯死,它们很快也完蛋了。There is a lot of truth in the saying 'No hide, no fur', proven this time by the fact that the pests met their death with gratifying swiftness (gratifying for me and for the tree) after free-falling to the ground, piggybacked on the purposefully discarded leaves and branches, and languishing with their dried-up food.

初夏,虫害季节已过,我的香椿树笑迎第二次生命,虽然依然形影相吊,但不再黯然孑立,而是开始生机勃发,亭亭玉立了。The Xiangchun's rebirth coincided with the vibrancy of early summer when the pest season was over. Though still by itself, it was no longer the picture of solitary melancholy. What we saw instead was a life rekindled, standing tall and proud.

就这样,一棵香椿树,凭它的智慧和坚忍,打赢了一场生死战。That is how a *Toona sinensis*, a fragrant tree of eternal spring, triumphed in mortal combat against all odds, with intelligence and perseverance.

Leonoir and Gingerlet 伙伴行

有肉不欢　One Man's Meat Is Leonoir's Poison

花了不少篇幅说完"污瓜"和香椿树的故事，现在回过头来接着说黑狮和小黄的各种"趣"事。Let me now return to the (sometimes) weird and (always) wonderful tales of Leonoir and Gingerlet after this meandering thematic detour that made pit stops at a certain melon of ignoble origin and a certain toon tree of noble intelligence. 既然说到植物，我不能不提起黑狮非常奇特的饮食习惯：他是素食主义者！小黄在家里，貌似也吃斋，只要我们给他白米粥和一些简单的蔬菜，他就很满意了，吃得倍儿香，但他毕竟每天自己捉鱼吃，那算是荤菜吧？所以他最多能声称"我不吃红肉"，实在是无法高攀素食主义这个华丽的时尚概念。Speaking of plants, it would be remiss of me not to mention Leonoir's very peculiar diet: He was a vegetarian! In fact, vegan would not be a misnomer for him either. Gingerlet might have appeared to be a herbivore too, pigging out on rice congee and greens with great gusto, but he caught and ate fish on a daily basis. He might have been justified to proclaim: 'I don't eat red meat.' But he was not a fashionable vegetarian by any stretch of the imagination.

黑狮刚到我家时，我们根据"常识"，喂肉骨头给他吃。When Leonoir first joined us, we were persuaded by 'common sense' to offer him pork bones. 他嗅了嗅，抬头看着我们，尾巴摇个不停，意思是："谢谢你们，但我不吃这个。"He took a sniff and looked up at us. His eyes and his wagging tail were saying, 'Thank you, but no thank you.' 我们以为他不爱生吃骨头，就把骨头烧熟了再给他吃。他又嗅了嗅，舔了舔，然后张开嘴将骨头咬住了。We thought raw food wasn't his cup of tea, so we cooked the bones and served them to him again. He sniffed and licked them and held one of them in his mouth. 但接下来他碰到了新的瓶颈：啃不动！我们从来没听说过这世上还有啃不动肉骨头的狗，后来这更

是成为左邻右舍流传的一个笑话。那个时代，肉类食品属于珍馐，凭票供应，小动物如果能尝到一点肉星儿，应该感激涕零才对呀。But the story didn't end here. His first bone-crunching attempt was foiled by a new challenge: The bones were too hard for him to crack. That was certainly news to us and later became a cause of hilarity among our neighbours who also kept dogs. In those days, meat was a rarity, subject to rationing. It was something pets would die for. 而且他根本不上心，敷衍地啃咬一番，觉得咬不动，就放弃了。心肠软得一塌糊涂的父亲拿来锤子，把骨头敲成小块，他总算勉强连嚼带吞，吃下去了。But Leonoir half-heartedly clacked his teeth on the bones, instead of sinking his teeth into them, and gave up as soon as his canine 'canines' and molars felt the resistance from the hardened hydroxyapatite. My father, soft-hearted to a fault, fetched his hammer, shattered the bones into more manageable shards and let Leonoir try again. It worked this time, as Leonoir was able to gulp them down without too much effort, but still with a palpable degree of reluctance.

  几个月后，我们才真正明白，黑狮对荤食本来就不感冒，加上肉骨头还要使劲儿嚼才能吃下去，为了自己不爱吃的东西还费那么大的劲，何苦来哉？我们设身处地一想，就理解了。It was not till a few months later that we finally understood Leonoir's dietary preferences. He was never into meat in the first place and the effort required to break and eat the bones made it an even less meaningful undertaking. Why would one go into so much trouble for something that one doesn't even fancy? It took quite a bit of empathy on our part to climb up the learning curve and appreciate his dilemma. 而另一方面，黑狮又具备典型的犬类性格，对主人竭尽献媚之能事，为了不让我们失望，我们给他吃的东西，他哪怕不想吃，也会装出很爱吃的样子，尾巴摇得很起劲，带动大半个身子左右摆动，眼神透出无尽的感激之情，为了掩饰自己的真实感受而倍加谄媚。Yet on the other hand, Leonoir was very much a dog in that he would do anything to keep his masters happy. He was always mindful not

Leonoir and Gingerlet 伙伴行

to disappoint us. Even if what we had offered him was not to his taste, all we saw was a grateful dog who found the food so yummy that nothing less than a mighty wag of his tail and an enthusiastic outpouring of his gratitude through his eyes would suffice to express his appreciation. It verged on sycophancy, to compensate for his suppressed real feeling about the food. 但我慢慢识破了他的表演，可以根据他张嘴咬下去的速度和力度，判断他是否真的爱吃。But he couldn't fool me for very long. In time, I was able to read the telltale signs that he was trying to mask with deliberation. Was he genuinely relishing his food or just pretending to like it? The answer lay in the speed and force with which he bit into it.

我母亲在单位里告诉同事，说家里有一条素食犬，同事不相信，说是天方夜谭，问我母亲敢不敢让他们试验一下，母亲胸有成竹地说："没问题，尽管放马过来！" When my mother told her colleagues that we had a canine vegetarian at home, nobody believed her. They said it sounded like a fanciful yarn inspired by *One Thousand and One Nights*. They challenged my mother by proposing a test for Leonoir. She agreed without hesitation, confident that Leonoir would not let her down. 'By all means. Just bring it on!' she said. 一天，母亲让黑狮尾随她上班，有位同事已经买好了一个肉包子、一个麻团，放在地上迎接黑狮。中国有句谚语："肉包子打狗——有去无回。"难道真的有例外？所有的同事都围过来，好戏开场了！One day, mother gave Leonoir permission to follow her to work. One of the colleagues had laid out a *roubaozi* and a *matuan* on the floor to greet him with. *Roubaozi* is a steamed bun with a pork filling (*rou* means meat in general and pork in particular in the region where I grew up; *baozi* means steamed bun with a filling). *Matuan* doesn't need explaining now, does it? That's right. It's the Chinese answer to doughnut, made from sticky rice flour typically filled with treacle and coated in sesame seeds... when sesame seeds are available, that is (remember our in-joke?). That a dog would go for *matuan* instead of *rou-*

baozi when presented with both at the same time was unheard-of. In fact, it is a truism to the Chinese mind that if you wish to repel a ferocious dog, don't hit it with a *roubaozi*, for he would be only too happy to accept it. Does this rule, like all rules, have an exception? A crowd gathered around. The show was on!

黑狮亮相了。他先是摇尾,向我母亲的那位同事致谢,然后开始用嗅觉辨别这两种食物的可口程度。他先嗅了嗅肉包子,迟疑片刻,抬头看了一眼那位同事,同时用眼角飞快地瞄了瞄周围的观众……我母亲知道他的心理活动:"这么多人捧场,我别太过分。"Entered Leonoir, star of the hour. He began by gesturing his appreciation with his tail. He then went on to start reconnoitring the two delicacies with his scent detector. He sniffed the *roubaozi* first. He paused, looked up at his benefactor while gathering the crowd into his field of vision by swiftly and almost imperceptibly rolling his eyes sideways, and decided to humour them to an extent that was acceptable to himself (this thought process being known to my mother only). 在众目睽睽之下,他低头轻轻咬破包子皮,在牙齿和舌头的协调下,熟练地将破了一个大洞的包子皮叼在嘴里,再轻轻一抖,里面的肉馅儿(当地人叫肉坨儿)滚到地上,包子皮他两三口就吃掉了,肉馅儿他看都没看。While being gawped at by a ring of spectators with bated breath, he pierced the wrapping with a dainty little bite and worked his tongue in coordination with his teeth to somehow manoeuvre the pork filling out of the dough. With a gentle shake of his head, the meatball rolled onto the floor. The *rou* was out; only the *baozi* skin remained in his mouth, which he quickly ate. The meatball didn't even get another look from him. 再转战麻团,这次他就不犹豫了,立即大嚼起来。麻团很黏,他吃得太快,只得时不时停下来,用舌头在嘴里理一理搅成一团乱麻的麻团。He then moved on to the matuan and, oh boy, was he in his element! He munched with such gusto that he had to stop now and then to untangle the sticky mess clinging to his palate, teeth and tongue.

这下子看热闹的观众全呆住了，他们都不敢相信自己的眼睛。The spectators, agog with curiosity, were now a crowd agape with disbelief. 黑狮一鸣惊人，以茹素狗的身份在当地一举成名！This atypical circus show, of grandstanding calibre, made Leonoir an instant celebrity in the local community.

藏宝记　If You Can't Eat It, Bury It

　　某个夏日的傍晚,我们在院子里吃晚饭,家常三样:白粥、红烧豇豆、咸鸭蛋。One summer evening, we were having supper on the patio. It was simple fare: plain rice congee, braised cowpeas and salted duck eggs. 我用筷子挑出两根豇豆,扔在地上给黑狮吃,他一吸溜就下肚了,显然很爱吃,吃完舔一下嘴,抬头继续盯着我看:"主人,再给我来点儿吧?" I picked up two cowpea pods with my chopsticks and put them on the ground for Leonoir to eat. He lapped them up and slurped them down in a single gulp. Obviously he loved cowpeas. A quick lick of his snout was followed by resumed gazing at his master, as if saying, 'Please, sir, I want some more.' 吃咸鸭蛋一般是把大头的蛋壳敲碎、剥去,用筷子掏着吃。It may be necessary to explain how we normally eat a salted duck egg in China: You crush the large end of the shell, pick the broken bits off and use that end to gain access to, and excavate, the white and the yolk with chopsticks, much like how Westerners tackle a hard-boiled egg at breakfast, minus the egg cup and the spoon. 那天我先把蛋黄吃掉了,嫌蛋白太咸且嚼之无味,就把剩下的部分连蛋壳丢给了黑狮。I ate the yolk of the salted duck egg. I found the white tasteless other than being too salty, so I offered the half empty shell to Leonoir. 黑狮照例舌鼻并用,先考察一番这个圆溜溜的新玩意儿。Leonoir, as usual, employed a combination of nose and tongue to investigate the edibility of the interestingly shaped novel object. 接着,他慢慢垂下舌头,轻轻舔了一下蛋壳开口处的边缘,"浅尝辄止",瞟了我一眼,见我正看着他,不得已低下头,硬着头皮又舔了一下。He then lolled his tongue out, slowly, and gave the edge of the hole in the shell a tentative lick. That was enough for him. He stopped and stole a glance at me. Realising that I was still looking at him, he decided to give this unpalatable 'delicacy' another chance. He licked again, with patent hesitancy. 我看出来了，他不爱吃这种"美味"，我当然不会强迫他吃不爱吃的东西，"己所不欲勿施于人"嘛。但我很好奇，心想："嘿嘿，且看你怎么办！" I could tell that he didn't care for the viand I had offered. That much was obvious. Of course I wasn't going to coerce him into eating what he didn't fancy. 'Do not impose on others what you yourself do not desire.' But I was also curious to see how he was going to handle this situation. 突然，他抬起头来，只见那个鸭蛋壳套在了他的下巴上——乌黑的脑袋白口罩！我"噗嗤"笑出声来，他立即变得非常兴奋，因为他知道，这一招奏效了，尴尬的僵局打破了。Suddenly, he looked up... Lo and behold, his lower jaw was now gloved with the egg shell, white on black! That was just too funny. I was in stitches, at which point he became very excited because he knew his trick had worked and he had broken the awkward silence. 他像一个带着面具的小丑，也像刚刚夺魁的运动员，把饭桌当作体育场，绕场狂奔接受欢呼，我父母看到他这么滑稽的样子，也忍不住笑了起来。他们一笑，黑狮就更来劲了。The masked clown started running frenetically in circles round our table, like an ecstatic, arm-flailing and national flag-waving Olympic running champion on a victory lap, spurred on by my parents' mirth at this hysterical scene. 黑狮就这样癫狂了一阵之后，向屋后跑去，消失了。After a spate of merry-go-round by this madcap (or madmask, rather) merrymaker, he disappeared behind the house. 过了几分钟，他又跑回来了，下巴上的鸭蛋壳不见了，给我的感觉是，他跑到屋后安静之处，把主人赐给他的美食全吃了。他在我面前再次坐下，一脸无辜地看着我，等着我下一轮的施舍。A few minutes later, he came back with his lower jaw unmasked, the egg shell nowhere to be seen, giving me the impression that he had gratefully gobbled up the goody in the quiet of that space behind the house. He sat down again before me and started staring at me, looking all innocent and waiting for my next bestowal.

但我不相信他把咸鸭蛋白给吃了，他之前的表情以及那个表情透露的他对咸鸭蛋的态度,我可是看得一清二楚的。I didn't buy the story he was trying to sell me, that he had eaten the salted egg white. He had found it repulsive when he first sniffed it. I could tell from his expression. 我到屋后转了一圈,没看见蛋壳,虽然心存疑窦,但也无话可说。黑狮跟着我,他那眼神的意思是:"你看,没有吧?我全吃了。" I got up and went round the back of the house. Leonoir followed me. I couldn't see the egg shell anywhere. I had to give him the benefit of the doubt. He said to me with his eyes, 'You see, I did eat it all.'

　　第二天,同样的场景。我把只剩下蛋白的咸鸭蛋连壳给了他,他熟练地套在下巴上,欢快地跑上两圈,逗我们笑笑,然后溜了。The next day, the same thing happened. I gave him the egg shell with all the egg white in it. He put it on his lower jaw, now with perfect ease. He frolicked round the table a couple of times to make us laugh. Then he ran off. 我立即悄悄跟上,偷看他到底是怎么处理的。I followed him surreptitiously to spy on him, to find out what he was going to do with it.

　　为了不被他发现,我在后墙那里停下,用墙壁挡住我的身体,只探出半个脑袋观察。I didn't want him to see me, so I hid myself behind the wall and stuck my head out. 只见黑狮衔着蛋壳,跑到离香椿树不远的地方,开始"双手"并用,刨坑！I saw Leonoir trotting to a spot not far from the Xiangchun tree. His lower jaw still sheathed in the egg shell, he started digging with both his hands. He was making a hole in the ground. 当然他不是尼尔森,这个挖掘工程不是为了挖出一个临时茅坑,他虽然吃饭蛮讲究的,但其他方面要求没那么高。Of course he was no Nelson the soldier. He wasn't undertaking this civil engineering project to construct a makeshift shit pit as Nelson did. He was less particular about his bodily functions than about his food.

　　他只花了几十秒,一个小坑就挖好了,他用嘴把鸭蛋壳放进去,然后转体180度,屁股对着埋葬咸鸭蛋的墓穴,"两手"把周围的泥土往后扒,两脚再以接力的方式,把这些泥土蹬进那个坑,掩埋蛋壳。It took him less than a minute to make that pit. He lowered the egg shell into the burial site and then turned round. He clawed back the earth that banked the shallow grave and his hind legs then pushed the earth back into the small vault. The salted duck egg shell was thus entombed. 在他工程快结束时，我立即抽身离开了，他一直不知道我目睹了那一幕，我也不忍心戳穿他精心编造的那个善意的谎言。I left promptly just before his work was done. He didn't find out I had witnessed the excavation and the burial, for I had not the heart to expose his meticulously fabricated white lie.

罗汉斋　A Monk's Diet

了解了黑狮的口味比较清淡，就好办了。我们开始让他品尝各种蔬果，最后发现他最爱吃的只有三样：南瓜、菱角、冬瓜！ Having established Leonoir's rather lean dietary leanings, we began offering him whatever fruits and vegetables were available to us. In time, we were able to whittle down a long list of possible favourites to just three: pumpkin, water caltrop and white gourd (aka winter melon). A few explanatory words on this exotic-sounding water caltrop are in order, I believe. It looks like this:

Leonoir and Gingerlet　伙伴行

In the West, people often call it water chestnut, but the same name is also given to the fruit of another plant, *Eleocharis dulcis*, which looks like this: Yes, water caltrop tastes like a chestnut (in fact, more so than its namesake because it's more starchy, less juicy) and it does grow in water, but it's much rarer in the Western world. When Chinese restaurants in Europe say a certain dish on the menu contains water chestnut, you can bet your bottom dollar that they are talking about *Eleocharis dulcis* (*bichi* or *maati*), not water caltrop (*lingjiao* or *laoling*).

而在这罗汉素三样中,黑狮最依赖的是冬瓜,夏天要是连续两天吃不上冬瓜,就会无精打采,终日趴在那里,用无神疲乏的目光打量周遭的一切,对其他食物毫无胃口,这些都是轻度中暑的症状(母亲称之为"疰夏")。但只要吃上一碗冬瓜汤(冬瓜、水、一撮盐、几滴麻油),立马神清气爽,两只圆圆的小眼睛再度燃亮。So those were the triple goodies of Leonoir the Monk, and secret to his happiness. He was most dependent on white gourd. If he went without it for two days in a row in summer, he would feel out of sorts. We would find him, a shadow of his usual self, lying on his tummy all day long in a state of perpetual lassitude, watching the world go by through his blank, disinterested, lacklustre eyes. He would have no appetite for any other food. Those were symptomatic of a mild heat stroke. My mother called it by its equivalent in traditional Chinese medicine, which is more descriptive: summer malaise. But a bowl of white gourd soup (made with a pinch of salt and a few drops of sesame oil) later, he would perk up as if by magic and become his bright-eyed, bushy-tailed self again. Well, they don't call it 'winter melon' for no reason. Leonoir would have been a perfect patient to testify to its potency as an antidote to the bodily invasions of enfeebling summer heat.

到了9月,天气稍凉,我们家吃上菱角时,也是黑狮在我们脚边逡巡,等候主人慷慨施舍的时候。In September, when the weather had cooled down a little, we would be snacking on water caltrops (*lingjiao*).

Leonoir would make sure he was never too far away from us. He didn't want to miss our handsome handouts. 为何我们的施舍得"慷慨"一点呢？这跟他的"吃相"有关。他爱吃的东西，都是囫囵吞枣，从来不细嚼慢咽、咂舌品尝，"咕咚"一声，没了，跟小黄吞噬白粥有得一拼，所以要么不给，要给就得给几个，否则他给我们的眼神信号是："什么？您给我东西吃了吗？我没吃着。要不再试试？" Why did the handouts have to be 'handsome', you may wonder? This has something to do with the way he ate his food. If he found the food palatable, he would polish it off in a single gulp without chewing or *degusting* the delicacy. This was not unlike how Gingerlet scooped and gobbled up plain congee. That's why when we gave *lingjiao* to Leonoir, we couldn't be stingy and offer him one at a time. Otherwise it would land in his open mouth and go straight to his stomach. Half a second later, he would signal to us with his eyes: 'What was that? Did I miss something? Try again please.'

秋天也是我们（包括黑狮）大啖南瓜的时节。但即便我们很慷慨，也无法满足他的胃口，邻居家的南瓜鸡食也成了他觊觎的对象。After snacking on water caltrops came feasting on pumpkins, later in autumn. But despite our generosity, Leonoir just couldn't have enough of them. He would go so far as to covet our neighbour's pumpkin-based chicken feed. 邻居吴阿姨发现放在院子里的鸡食被黑狮偷吃了几次之后，没办法，就把鸡食盆塞进狭小的鸡窝，让鸡在室内用餐。我当时想：鸡有夜盲症，鸡窝里又没有烛光，摸黑吃饭，挺不容易的。After Leonoir pulled off a number of pumpkin thefts in Auntie Wu's yard, she had no choice but to push the bowl into her chickens' little hut and let them eat in peace while cooped up in the coop. A cosy candle-lit dinner (minus the candles) in the comfort of one's home may sound romantic, but I'm sure it was no fun for the chickens with the kind of visual handicap that is named after their species.

有天早上，黑狮再度被举报。"他居然把头伸进鸡窝，把南瓜吃光了，还把鸡窝拱坏了！"吴阿姨反映。But one morning, he was at it again, according to Auntie Wu. 'He stuck his head in the hen house and finished all the pumpkin! And to top it all, he even vandalised the hen house!' 母亲向她连连道歉:"对不起,对不起,他真是狗胆包天,屡教不改! 我去骂他。那鸡窝,要不要让老季帮你修一修?" My mortified mother apologised repeatedly, 'I am terribly sorry. The nerve of him! And incorrigible! I'll tell him off. My husband could help you mend the hen house. Would you like that?' 母亲这么一说,吴阿姨的气也就消了,说不用麻烦老季了,她先生老刘可以弄好。The apoplectic Wu backed off. She said it was okay and her husband could see about the trashed avian property. 就这样,黑狮被骂了一顿,后来如何,我不记得了,也许他觉得偷吃南瓜有损自己的形象,戒了,也许刘伯伯加强了防范,反正好像相安无事了。So Leonoir received another reprimand. What happened after that? I don't remember. What I do remember is that there were no more complaints from Wu. Maybe Leonoir came to realise that this misdemeanour was unworthy of him and his sense of dignity prevailed. Or, perhaps, Wu's husband somehow shored up their defences.

"攀"比　Getting a Cat's Eye View

　　黑狮口味素净，看门却一点不含糊，而且无师自通。他有两大绝招：一是叫声震天，二是奔跑极快。这两招都能让他的敌人猛吃一惊，乱了阵脚。Having a taste for veggies did not make Leonoir a namby-pamby when it came to performing his watchdog duties. Although we never schooled him to be a fit-for-purpose K9 vigilante, he excelled in that profession thanks to his two outstanding gifts: He was an exceptionally loud barker and an exceptionally fast runner. He could take his enemies by surprise, discombobulate them and render them defenceless. 我母亲就曾经在城里听到两个陌生人在议论，说城北养殖场那里有条黑狗很凶很疯，怪吓人的，她这才知道，黑狮已经声名远扬了。Once my mother overheard a conversation between two strangers in town. They were discussing a very 'aggressive' black dog acting like a loose cannon, in the fish farm area. 'Wow, our dog's reputation precedes him,' she thought to herself.

　　在家里，黑狮对主人俯首帖耳，为了讨主人的欢心，上刀山，下火海，在所不惜，但对小黄的感情却比较复杂，一方面他把小黄当弟弟对待，在必要时毫不犹豫地保护他（例如小黄爬树时，他就会把邻居家的黑腹狗小丽赶走，防止她利用小黄从树上下来，站立不稳的时机欺负他）。另一方面呢，又觉得小黄辈分比自己低，却更加得宠，有特制的窝，可以上桌，上其他高于地面的地方，时不时还能在我们怀里或腿上打呼噜。At home, Leonoir was every bit a devoted and obliging canine companion. He would jump through any number of hoops to keep his masters happy. No complaints there. But he was ambivalent about Gingerlet, equal parts loving and resentful towards him. He did see Gingerlet as his little brother and would stick his neck out for Gingerlet without hesitation, if called for. He would, for instance, chase away *Xiao Li* (Little Pret-

Leonoir and Gingerlet 伙伴行

ty), a scheming, cowardly and bullying excuse of a dog kept by another neighbour, when Gingerlet was practising tree climbing. *Xiao Li* had been seen trying to hurt Gingerlet when he was in a vulnerable position during the climb down. On the other hand, from Leonoir's perspective, Gingerlet was his junior, an under-cat if you like, on a lower rung of the pecking order, and yet seemed to get more attention from us. Let's face it, Gingerlet had a purpose-built nest all to himself. He was allowed on the table and other raised surfaces. From time to time, he was seen getting purringly cosy in our arms or in our lap. 黑狮除了匍匐在我脚旁，或者站起来，前爪搭在我的膝盖上寻求关注，或者用叽叽咕咕、偶尔混入一两声低吠表示"我也要"之外，没有其他办法，觉得很委屈。Apart from grovelling at my feet, pawing at my knees for attention, whimpering or grumbling 'Why can't I have the same', accentuated with an occasional muted bark or two, there was very little Leonoir could do. He felt slighted. 他按捺不住自己的嫉妒心、好奇心，想方设法去体验小黄的视角。他克服了恐高症，抓住机会登高远眺。But at some point, his jealousy and curiosity got the better of him. He even overcame his acrophobia just to experience Gingerlet's perspective from an elevated point. 有几次父母出门时，把黑狮反锁在屋里了，他无法出去轰轰烈烈地迎接我放学。我走向家门口时，远远看见窗户里，在桌面的高度游荡着两盏小灯，贼亮的。我一看就知道，那是黑狮的眼睛，屋里很暗，黑狮又是"黑"狮，有天然的保护色，所以除了那双眼睛暴露了他的所在之外，并无其他破绽。There were a number of occasions when my parents locked Leonoir in the house, intentionally or unawares. He couldn't get out to welcome me home with the usual pomp and circumstance. As I was walking along the equivalent of a driveway towards the front door, I saw a couple of tiny 'lights' through the window. The shiny dots were hovering at the level of the tabletop. I knew instantly that they were Leonoir's eyes. It was dark inside the house. Leonoir, being *noir*, blended in with the dark background. But he fell short of being completely invisible: His inconveniently bright eyes betrayed his exact location. 就在我看到他的那个瞬间，他也看到我了，然后那两盏灯就不见了——他慌忙跳下了桌子。He also saw me when I saw him. A split second later, the pair of lights disappeared. He had scurried off the table.

我进门后，黑狮照例对我表示热烈欢迎，但与此同时，他的身体语言似乎多了一层含义。My entry into the house met with Leonoir's signature reception, but there was something else in his body language. 他先用眼睛捉住我的目光，再用眼神向我示意，同时向屋子的另一侧迈出去两步，然后回到原点，如此重复多次，意思是："您别去桌子那里，您跟我到别处去玩吧！" His eyes engaged mine and started cueing me as to where I should be going, i.e. away from the table. To make that signal more explicit, he turned his body halfway towards the other side of the room, took a couple of steps in that direction and then returned to the original spot. He repeated it a few times. The message was loud and clear: 'Please move away from the table. Let's play over there, shall we?'

我扫了一眼桌子……哈哈，原来桌上留下了他的"爪纹"！I scanned the table. Guess what? He had left his paw-prints on the surface! 我一点都没生气，一来觉得他笨拙得可笑、可爱，二来惊叹他的智力，他显然知道自己肯定在犯罪现场留下了罪证，没来得及销毁（可能也不知道怎么销毁），所以想转移我的注意力，让我发现不了。I wasn't cross with him at all. How could I possibly get mad at such amusing, endearing clumsiness? Besides, I had to take my hat off to his intelligence. Obviously, he was vaguely aware he had left some incriminating evidence at the crime scene and that he had not had the time (or criminal savvy) to give the table a once-over, which explains his attempt to distract me and discourage me from getting near that spot.

Leonoir and Gingerlet   伙伴行

地盘争夺战　**Turf War**

　　黑狮对小黄的嫉妒和攀比心态，不仅体现在登高上。在我们不注意时，他也会做些小动作，为难小黄。So Leonoir wanted to have what Gingerlet had and developed the un-canine habit of getting up high to keep up with the Joneses. But his jealousy and competitiveness didn't stop there. Sometimes, he would play little tricks, when we were not looking, to inconvenience Gingerlet. 例如，黑狮胃口不好时，看着小黄喝粥时狼吞虎咽的吃相就气不打一处来，就像失眠者看到他人呼呼大睡那样，但又不能拦住他，让他别吃。怎么办呢？只能使点坏，让他无法吃得尽兴，也能解解气。你跑不过人家，就使个绊子呗。For example, if Leonoir didn't have much of an appetite, he would find the way Gingerlet stuffed himself with congee quite irritating. Insomniacs in the company of snorers can relate to that, can't they? He couldn't tell Gingerlet to stop, naturally, but he could throw a wrench in the works to prevent Gingerlet from eating to his heart's content. If you cannot outrun someone, trip him up.

　　黑狮使出的法宝就是他的体重！他虽然不是一条大狗，但很敦实，身体相当沉，这是他对付小黄的一个明显优势。He needed a tool to pull his tricks off and that tool was his body weight. He wasn't big for a dog, but his stocky body was pretty heavy, which gave him a clear advantage over Gingerlet. 他的碗和小黄的碗并排放着，他就利用这个机会，挤到小黄身边，假装在自己碗里吃东西，然后一点一点挪动身子，把小黄往旁边挤，小黄避让，接着吃，他就得寸进尺，直到他"占着猫碗不吃饭"，直到小黄放弃抵抗，抽身离去，到一旁洗脸去为止。Their bowls were next to each other. He would inch ever closer to Gingerlet while pretending to be eating from his own bowl. Slowly, he would bulldoze Gingerlet to the side. Without giving up eating, the big-hearted Gingerlet would quietly move aside a little to make room for him. But Leonoir would continue muscling Gingerlet out of the way until he couldn't reach his bowl any more, at which point Gingerlet would stop eating, walk away and start his grooming session. A classic case of dog in the (cat's) manger!

黑狮虽然不是技穷的黔驴,但他的花招确实也不多,一招奏效后,他就会在其他场合如法炮制。While Leonoir was more resourceful than a one-trick pony, he didn't really have a large repertoire of game plans. If one move had rewarded him with one-upmanship over Gingerlet, he would try using it again in another situation.

冬天,黑狮和小黄都喜欢在正门的门槛上晒太阳,因为正门朝南,全天日照时间最长,而且门槛是"里"和"外"的分界点,坐在门槛上,温暖安逸的家在后方,洒满阳光的庭院和外面精彩的世界也能尽收眼底。In winter, both Leonoir and Gingerlet enjoyed sunbathing on the threshold of the front door. The south-facing façade benefited from the longest exposure to daytime sunlight. The threshold was the boundary line between 'inside' and 'outside'. Sitting on the threshold, they had the comfort of their home behind them and a near-panoramic view of all the exciting goings-on out there, on the sun-drenched patio and beyond.

我家的正门就是普通的单扇门,不宽,因此门槛不长。Ours was a regular single door. The threshold, therefore, was not very long. 如果小黄靠着门枢那侧在门槛上坐下的话,剩余的部分让我们进出,宽度正好,这时候如果黑狮再跟他排排坐,就会挡道,就会被我们赶走。如果他赖在那里不动,我们进出屋子时,脚就会在他脑袋上刮来蹭去,他很快就受不了了,只得悻悻然起身,走到院子里,找个暂栖点,凑合着趴下来继续补充维生素D。If Gingerlet got there first and parked himself on the threshold, his body leaning against the hinge side, there would be enough space for us to pass through. But if Leonoir decided to sit with him side by side, he would be blocking our way and would be told to move over. If he refused to budge, our feet would inadvertently skim his

Leonoir and Gingerlet 伙伴行

head, from time to time, as we stepped over him. Serving as a doormat was obviously humiliating and frustrating for him, so after a while, he would, sullen-faced, concede that he had been turfed out and would get up to stay out of harm's way. He would walk around a little and eventually find a less desirable *pied-à-terre* in the yard to continue his Vitamin D therapy.

有一天，小黄再次捷足先登，占据了门槛上那几寸宽的黄金地盘。One day, Leonoir was once again pipped at the post by Gingerlet, who ensconced himself on the only lounge-friendly part of the threshold, several inches wide. 黑狮很恼火，但又不能当着我们的面把小黄赶走，只好将就着在他旁边先坐下。不知情的人只会看见阳光在他们的身后投下了一幅"哥俩好"的温馨剪影。Though annoyed, Leonoir held himself back, knowing we were watching. He had to settle for that same old inconvenient section of the threshold next to Gingerlet. If you were not privy to the dynamics between these two creatures, you would be forgiven to think, at first blush, that you were witnessing a ringing endorsement of brotherhood in the shape of a silhouette, projected onto the floor behind, of a cat and a dog 'rubbing shoulders' with each other and luxuriating in the blissful sunshine of fraternal love. 但你要是继续观察的话，就会看到剪影中哥哥笨重的身体开始向弟弟渐渐倾斜、压迫。The same silhouette, if observed any further, would show some slo-mo change of structure, with the big brother's oafish shadow leaning towards, and closing in on, that of the younger brother. 与此同时，弟弟的身影开始缩小，到最后哥哥的影子跟门框、门槛构成了三角形，而弟弟就成了卡在三角形里的一个球状物。The latter would begin to shrink, in tandem with the canine shadow looming menacingly large by comparison, and would eventually turn into a much smaller hard-pressed blob, trapped inside the triangle formed by the big brother, the jamb and the threshold. 这个变化持续下去的结果，就是小黄被挤得太难受了，他也知道，这样近身格斗，他不是黑狮的对手，因此不得不在这场综合格斗的地面攻

防战中认输，逃之夭夭，这时黑狮就会把屁股挪过去，心安理得地占下那块风水宝地。This process would continue until Gingerlet couldn't take it any more. He wasn't ready to punch above his weight, so he would tap out in this bout of MMA ground fighting and abandon the much-coveted prime spot under duress, whereupon Leonoir would shift his butt over to reclaim this territory, feeling no qualms whatsoever.

侠客传奇　Dr Peace Lover and Mr Rat Hunter

争夺地盘的过程中，小黄基本上都是逆来顺受，不太像普通人心目中的猫。总的来说，兄弟俩之所以从未大打出手，主要归功于小黄。他平时脾气也很好，毫无猫老爷的乖戾之气。Gingerlet was a cat alright, but in the turf war, he behaved quite unlike the old-school cat. He took things as they came, by and large, without getting all 'catty' at the slightest provocation. One might as well call him a pushover, very much the opposite of a 'grumpy cat'. I would give him most of the credit for the fact that they were never at each other's throats. 但他这种性格，在捉老鼠时便荡然无存，让人觉得他平时韬光养晦，碰到家庭内部矛盾，也是能忍则忍，目的就是为了在关键时刻一招制敌！But Gingerlet was no slouch when he was on the prowl. The docile side in him would vanish the moment he saw a rat, by which I mean one of those ginormous nasty rats, not teeny-weeny pettable mice. By the looks of it, he was conserving his energy when there was no battle to fight, even if his brother Leonoir was trying to pick a fight with him out of boredom or jealousy. But when the moment came, when he could prove his real worth, when his unique skills really mattered, he would rise to the occasion and subdue his foe in one fell swoop!

猫科动物以极强的爆发力和灵活敏捷著称，例如猎豹的杀手锏就是短跑快（比博尔特快两倍半）、变速快（其加速度是人类的四倍，而"急刹车"时每一步的减速幅度高达每小时14公里），简直就是动物王国里的碳纤维赛车。The cat family, including members of varying sizes, is known for their explosive muscle power and agility. For example, cheetahs famously apply their astounding sprinting velocity (two and a half times faster than Usain Bolt's) and swift speed variation (accelerating four times faster than humans and decelerating by just under nine miles per hour in a single stride) to subject their prey to a double whammy. In that sense, they are the carbon fibre racing cars of the animal kingdom. 家猫捉老鼠时,也必须发挥这两项特长,因为他们的猎物在"鼠窜"时,靠的是变幻多端的迷魂步把天敌甩掉。When domestic cats are in hot pursuit, they must bring into play the same lethal combination to make sure that the scampering rats, which rely on zigzag foxtrot to throw their hunters off course, will not succeed.

有一天,我亲眼目睹了小黄的身手,虽然早就知道他武功非凡,但还是不敢相信自己的眼睛,时至今日,那个考验小黄爆发力的瞬间,在我记忆中,依然似梦非梦。One day, I witnessed Gingerlet's feline prowess in action. I hadn't been unaware of the sort of explosive power he might have, but when it was actually put on display, I began to doubt my eyes. To this day, whenever I recall that moment, the moment when Gingerlet was really put through his paces, there is still a surreal feel to it. 那天傍晚,一只老鼠不知从哪儿突然冒了出来,它看到小黄,愣了一下,立即掉转头,一溜烟儿地跑了。It was early evening. A rat suddenly appeared from nowhere. It saw Gingerlet, froze for a split second, turned tail and scuttered away. 当然,这只老鼠的出现,不可能逃过小黄那双专为昏暗的光线中发现"动"物而设计的眼睛,他毫不犹豫,像旋风一样扑将过去。"猫捉耗子"的劲爆秀就开场了！Nothing that moved could have escaped Gingerlet's eyes, which were biologically wired to detect 'animated' objects in the dark. There was not a moment to lose. He whizzed past me and sprang at the fleeing target. Thus began a breathtaking 'cat-and-mouse' chase.

小黄很快缩短了跟老鼠之间的距离,逼着老鼠只能沿着直线发足狂奔,根本无法施展凌波微步了。Before long, Gingerlet began to gain on the rat, forcing it to follow a straight line, as it had no room or time to weave its way forward in the fashion of the fabled arrow-dodging swashbucklers. 老鼠冲到了前面人家的后墙,终于可以使出鼠类必胜技:轻功攀墙(又称"飞檐走壁")！The first sprinter made it to the back wall

Leonoir and Gingerlet 伙伴行

of the house in front of ours. It saw its chance. It was a perfect set-up for it to pull off its well-tested murine stunt: levitational wall climbing (aka parkour)! 它知道，自己虽然跑不过猫，但垂直攀爬速度，猫很可能不如自己。It knew full well that it would be outraced by the cat on level ground, but it had a good chance of beating the cat in the vertical leg of the obstacle course. 只见它不消两秒钟，就从地面爬到了两米高的屋檐那里，名副其实的"如履平地"。It took the rat less than two seconds to *walk* up the six-foot-tall wall and get to the eaves. 下一个瞬间，它就会钻进屋檐和墙顶之间的空隙，进入邻居家里，小黄就得"空爪而回"了。It was one second away from squeezing through the gap between the eaves and the top of the wall and disappearing into the neighbour's house, leaving Gingerlet empty-pawed. 小黄此时也冲到了墙根那里，抬头一看，心想："糟糕，我要是也爬上去的话，这小子肯定溜之大吉了！"Gingerlet had by now reached the foot of the wall. Looking up, he knew straight away that his prey was already out of reach, if he were to *climb* up the wall as well. 小黄接下来的举动把我看呆了，不亚于靠吊威亚和特技拍出来的动作片镜头。说时迟那时快，他气沉丹田，倏地一跃而起，"飞"到了离地两米的屋檐高度，只见他一手搭住一根椽子，一手将正在往缝里钻的老鼠扒拉了出来（武侠小说里的"轻舒猿臂"，恐怕就是指这种动作），往嘴里一塞，吊在屋檐上的手一松，轻轻飘落，着地后气定神闲，快步走出了院子。Time was of the essence. What happened in the next instant was like a scene straight out of an action thriller, shot with the help of wires and special effects. It was so fast and so incredible that my eyes struggled to take it all in. This is what I saw: Mustering his visceral power, Gingerlet's lithe body *lifted* off the ground and *rocketed* to the eaves in one clean hop. What does that mean? It means he cleared six or seven feet with a single push of his legs! Hanging from one set of claws nailed to one of the rafters, he grabbed the fugitive with his spare hand in the nick of time and stuffed it into his mouth. (What leaps to mind right now as I recall that epic moment is the iconic image of a caped swordsman holding onto the side of a hurtling train while taking on a dangerous villain with aplomb and eventually overpowering his nemesis.) That done, he retracted the equivalent of Captain Hook's metal prosthesis, landed like a feather and sped out of our yard the way a light-footed pixie would, without breaking a sweat. For him, the whole thing was just a walk in the park.

猫科动物虽然骁勇善战，但共同的短板是缺乏耐力，羚羊只要跟猎豹耗上几十秒，就有希望豹口脱险。但小黄与众不同，他的耐力也很惊人。While cats are generally acknowledged as some of the best fighters in the animal kingdom, they are also famously lacking in stamina. For example, an impala has a better-than-average chance of fleeing to safety if it can keep the formidable cheetah chasing for longer than a minute. But Gingerlet had more stamina than we had given him (and cats in general) credit for. Protracted battles were right up his street, too. 有时，我们早上一开门，就看见小黄正对着门，端坐在院子里，身旁一溜死耗子，有五六只之多，他是用这份礼物来向主人邀功。Sometimes, we would open our front door in the morning only to see Gingerlet sitting pretty in the yard, facing the door. By his side would lie a row of five or six rodent corpses. They represented his morning greetings to his masters. 我们当然要表扬他两句。他听了之后，旁顾左右，轻闭双眼，轻描淡写地"喵"一声："好说。知道你们不喜欢这些家伙，我就把他们收拾了一下，小意思。我自己不爱吃，我连鱼都吃腻了，但看你们一个个面黄肌瘦的，弄两只老鼠补补身子也蛮不错的嘛，何况这些都是小鲜肉，不是你们平时吃的那种恶心的腐肉！" Of course we would say 'thank you', 'bravo' or some such thing to him, to which he would reply with a nonchalant meow while looking away and squinting his eyes. By that meow, he was playing down the significance of his feat, 'You are welcome. I knew you found these rascals quite a bother, so I brought them into line. Easy-peasy. Besides, you look like you could do with some wholesome food to put some colour back in your faces, even though I don't fancy it myself. I have more than enough fish on my plate. Mind you, what you are looking at is tender fresh meat, not the disgusting carrion that you are used to eating.' 如果仔细观察这些老鼠，就会发现，它们都没有伤口，说明不是被小黄咬死的，而是被他"盘"死的。一夜能玩死五六只老鼠，足见小黄的耐力也是非同寻常的。A closer examination would reveal no visible sign of trauma on these dead bodies, which means they had not been bitten to death, but had died of exhaustion in Gingerlet's hunting games. That Gingerlet was able to *tease* up to six rats to death on a single spree speaks volumes for his astounding staying power.

义气   The Sanctity of Friendship

  小黄的生活，戎马倥偬，白天奔袭鱼类，晚上与硕鼠厮杀，偶尔还上蹿下跳企图捉拿小鸟，忙得不亦乐乎。Gingerlet's quotidian routine was an action-packed one featuring soldierly engagements: a blitzing fisher by day and a dashing rat terminator by night. And, occasionally, a committed but ineffective would-be bird catcher, in his futile attempts to defy gravity and the inborn handicap of non-avian creatures. 相反，黑狮的世界和谐多了，除了隔三差五地履行看家的职责、保护或欺负小黄外，他跟其他小动物的互动以游戏居多，举头赏鸟、低头观鱼，不拿耗子、不管闲事。By contrast, Leonoir set himself up in a much less confrontational world. He was by default a watchdog and as such, he did a sterling job discharging his duties, including that of deterring suspected intruders with aggression. Admittedly, he could be a horrid big brother to Gingerlet sometimes, bullying him now and again. But other than that, he spent most of his waking moments frolicking with smaller animals. For him, both birds and fish, in their aerial and underwater realms respectively, were to be admired from a distance. While rats did not deserve the same positive interest from him, catching them was not his business and he had no intention to engage in such thankless meddling.

  有一天晚上，我们家吃田鸡。那也是夏天，所以我们还是在院子里吃晚饭。我把吃剩的田鸡骨头扔到地上，给黑狮尝尝。One summer evening, we were having frogs for supper on the patio. I offered the frog bones to Leonoir to see if he was interested. 他摇尾致谢，走过去先嗅了一嗅。As usual, with an appreciative wag of his tail, he walked over to the bones and took a sniff. 忽然，他身体僵住了，毛发倒竖，连退三步，同时抬头看着我，似乎在向我求证什么。我在他放大的瞳孔里看到了极度的错愕。But what followed was totally unexpected: He was transfixed. His hair stood on end. He shuffled backwards and looked up at me, as if he couldn't believe what he had discovered and wondered if I knew it as well. I saw utter terror in his dilated pupils. 我问他，是不是真不想吃？他惊呆了，也顾不上讨好我（不像之前对咸鸭蛋的处理方法），一声不吭地走开了，让我百思不得其解。I asked him if he was sure that he didn't fancy it. He was clearly spooked and still in shock. Instead of humouring me in that 'needs must' way as he had done with the egg shells, he just walked off. I was left scratching my head.

几天后，我到屋后的鱼塘一带"执行任务"，这个"任务"我下面会说到。Some days later, I went on a 'mission' to scout the area dotted with fish ponds behind our house (more on that later). 老远看到黑狮在鱼塘边上来回跑动。他显得很开心，在一个很短的距离间一来一去、一来一去，像刘翔练习快速转向那样。I saw Leonoir in the distance running to and fro by one of the ponds. He seemed to be in his element. He kept shuttling between two points that were not far apart, like a runner practising quick turnabout. 他虽然在不断跑动，但眼睛却一直盯着地面上的某样东西。While he was moving about, his eyes were fixed on something on the ground. 我猫着腰，蹑手蹑脚，从侧面走近一点，定睛一看：草丛里有两只青蛙，正在欣赏黑狮的表演，它们给黑狮叫好的方式，就是时不时来几下蛙跳，惹得黑狮更加兴奋！I ducked down and tiptoed a little closer. What met my eyes were a couple of frogs in the grass! They were Leonoir's audience and they were a gracious lot. From time to time, they rewarded his entertaining shenanigans with some of their signature hops, only to send Leonoir into a bigger frenzy.

我把前后两件事联系起来一想，全明白了！I put two and two together and - 'eureka', the earlier mystery was solved！这么说吧，如果电视台宠物频道采访黑狮，请他对人类吃青蛙的行为发表看法，他会说："我跟青蛙是老朋友了，我们经常混在一起，他们太可爱了，也很幽默，我们玩得很开心。但主人居然把它们煮熟了吃，我的小主人还说，最好吃的做法是用毛豆炒田鸡腿，加几瓣蒜，用大火快炒，这样才鲜嫩可口（粤语叫"幼滑"）。太残忍了！我简直不敢相信自己的鼻子和眼睛！" Let me put it this way: If Leonoir had been approached by the Pet Channel to weigh in on (some) human beings' interest in grenouilles as food, he would have said, 'Frogs and I go way back. We often hang out together. They are adorable and humorous creatures. We have so much fun. But my masters cook them and eat them! And that's not all. My young master is quite particular about how they are cooked. His favourite recipe is sautéed succulent frog legs with fresh soybeans, flavoured with julienned ginger and a few cloves of raw garlic. He says this dish must be wokked on high heat to get the taste right! How can humans be so cruel, so twisted? I couldn't believe my eyes, or my nose.'

　　养宠物的人，也许有体会：动物的性格会对主人产生影响。起码我是这样的。Pet owners might agree with me that the 'personality' of their animals is contagious. Or maybe I am only speaking for myself. 我家的茹素狗、喝粥猫，就对我后来的饮食习惯似乎产生了很大的影响。For example, my taste in food seems to have been heavily influenced by the canine vegetarian and feline congee gourmet in my family. 这属于直接影响，还有一些间接影响，体现在其他方面，例如在我眼中，动物，不仅是哺乳类动物，都是跟我们差不多的，只是有的小一点，有的傻一点罢了。Apart from such direct influence, there are subtler manifestations of what my association with my pets has done to me. As far as I am concerned, animals - and not just mammals - are not that different from us. True, they may not be 'human', but they are not subhuman either. They may be littler than we are; they may be more clueless in areas where we are more knowledgeable. But that's about it.

Leonoir and Gingerlet 伙伴行

弹弓枪　Catapult Pistols

前面说到，我家屋后有几口鱼塘，我到那里执行过"任务"。那个任务的代号是"猎鸟行动"。I mentioned just now that I had gone on a mission round the fish ponds behind our house. The mission was code-named *Operation Birding*.

当时我自制了一把弹弓。我在家里翻出一小块皮革，好像是人造革吧，蛮硬的，我把它切成椭圆形，再拿来那个时代孩子们的至宝——橡皮筋，编成两股当时觉得威力很大的弹力绳，又从外面地上找来一根比较合适的树枝桠，用小刀（也是自制的）削巴削巴，就做成了挺称手的弹弓。I had made a hand catapult myself. The materials I used included a piece of scrap leather (or faux leather, because it wasn't as supple) I had found at home, cut into an oval shape; a short forked stick that I had crafted from a twig with a self-made knife; and two braids of rubber bands. It felt powerful in my hand and it was easy to hold. 那个时候的我，动手能力很强，不像现在，用进废退，已经丢功了。你也许猜到了，我是从小鹤那里沾到了一点工匠的灵气。I was quite the handyman in those days and as you might have guessed, the engineering talents of Xiao He had somehow rubbed off on me. (I hasten to add that work in the proverbial shed is no longer my strong suit. Practice makes perfect; disuse renders skills rusty.) 但这不是主要原因，我的匠艺（虽然不出众）是与生俱来的，因为我父亲是一位很有才华的多面手，是他给了我这方面的基因。But that wasn't the main reason. I wasn't born with a silver spoon in my mouth, but I did come to this world with a sliver of boon in my genetic makeup: My father was a Renaissance man, a DIY past master. 这里打个岔，2005年，我在博客中写了一段回忆我父亲的文字，当时是用英语写的，不是中英双语，现在原文照搬，我父亲的"手巧"，可见一斑。In that vein, I would like to quote an English blog I wrote back in 2005, about my father. The artisan *par excellence* in my father is patent in this story:

> Recently, I realised I don't have a 'hobby', something that I enjoy doing outside of work, something to kill time with that doesn't have a clear 'purpose'. Everything I do either relates to work or has a definable (usually 'good') purpose, martial arts included.
>
> I remember my father had a hobby, which he took up after he had emerged from a bad patch in his life. Now to think of it, he must have been deeply traumatised by that experience and developed that hobby as a healing balm for his scarred psyche. His other means of 'escape' was being with the fishermen, teaching them how to breed freshwater fish artificially, how to cultivate pearls and how to increase crab yield, among other things. He used to marvel at the untapped intelligence of fishermen's children and attributed their cerebral excellence to eating copious amounts of fish. He was later proven right, as scientific findings point to a correlation between the intake of sufficient phosphorus, which abounds in fish, and high IQ.
>
> His hobby, which I was referring to, was making miniature furniture, or scaled-down models of furniture. He would make minuscule parts from wood, fit them together (with sockets and dowels, instead of screws and nails), sand them down, paint over them (primed with a clear varnish first, then coated with a coloured paint) and lay a veneer over the top surface... i.e. everything that would go into a normal piece of furniture. He would then place the finished products on a table, scrutinise them every day to see where he could improve,

and go on to make better ones later on. He also started cooking more. He honed his culinary skills to perfection. He practically monopolised the kitchen. 'Get out of my way!' was his much-repeated mantra to hound me and my mother out of the kitchen.

宕开的一笔,弹回来接着说弹弓的故事。*Interlude over. Let me swing back to the slingshot.*

弹弓做好了,得试试吧?打墙靶没劲,早在弹弓枪流行时就玩腻了。我有几把弹弓枪,分为木制和铁质两种,都是父亲给我做的。*Once I had the catapult in my hand, I felt the urge to test it, but against what? I wasn't keen on aiming at a target fixed to the wall. I had been there, done that years before when catapult guns were all the rage. I had several rubber band-powered pistols in those days, made of either wood or wire. Their designer-cum-builder was none other than my father.* 木制弹弓枪就是把木块削成手枪形状,枪头拧上羊眼螺丝,后端用去头铁钉和铁丝做成"纸弹"夹和扳机机构。*The wooden ones consist of a block of wood in the shape of a pistol. A pair of screw eyes at the front of the barrel hold the rubber bands while a pair of headless nails keep the armed paper bullet in place. There is also a trigger, wrought with wire, that when squeezed levers the 'bullet' off the clamping nails and releases the tensioned projectile.* 要做铁质的弹弓枪,你得艺高手有力:左手一根铁丝,右手一把老虎钳(左撇子可以对调一下),其他什么都没有,若没有丰富的想象力,没有又巧又有劲的一双手,怎么做?*Making a wire pistol is more challenging though. You have to be a better craftsman with a highly creative mind. You have a wire in your left hand and a pair of pliers in your right (swap around if you are a southpaw) and whatever is lacking you make up for with your brain and your brawn.*

简单说一下"纸弹"的质地。*A few words about the paper ammunition.* 普通稿纸软硬适中,容易折叠,尖角有一定的刚性,被它打中还是挺疼的；香烟壳更硬，折出来的弹药更具"杀伤力"，但由于不易弯曲，只能做成又大又沉的子弹，皮筋儿力道不大的话，射程就大打折扣了；最低级的材料是草纸（正宗的"草"纸，黄色、多孔，吸水性太好……你懂的），软趴趴的，所谓的尖角只是形状，银样镴枪头，根本没有刺痛效果。Writing paper was the best material for making bullets, not too hard, not too soft. Folding was easy and the spur was rigid enough to deliver a painful sting. Cigarette pack paper (cardboard was not used for this purpose in those days), being stiffer, would produce more effective 'bullets', but you win some, you lose some: As it was less pliable, one would need a larger square for each bullet and the heftier product required more elastic power to catapult across the same range. A poor relation of those two options was the abrasive, highly absorbent (excessively so, to the point of jeopardising hand hygiene...) straw-based tissue that used to be the gold standard of toilet paper. The bullets so created were a disgrace to their name. The spur only looked like a peak, but was hopelessly peaky and could not cause any damage whatsoever. 我们当年没有那么多的纸

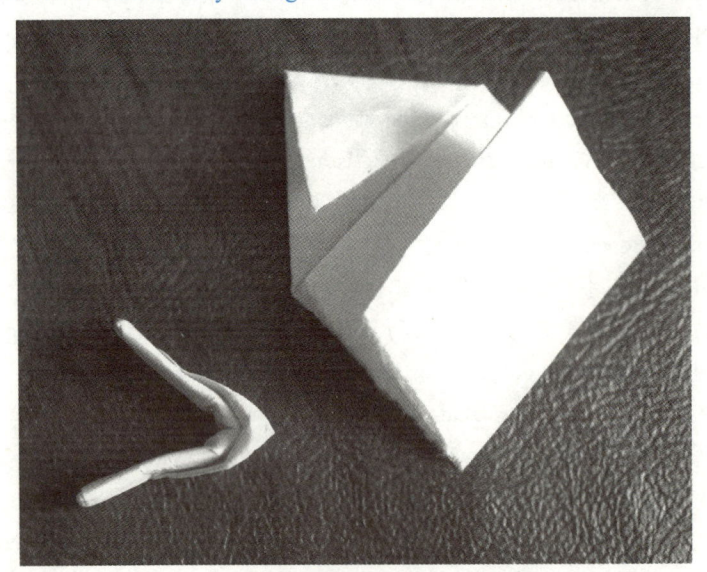

纸弹(摄影:梁子嫣)*A paper bullet.(photo by Lulu Liang)*

可用，所以打出去的纸弹，还得回收，从地上捡起来后用牙咬一咬，收紧后再用，反复使用的次数多了，这些弹药就被口水泡软了，最后打出去的不是挺括的纸弹，而是奇形怪状的纸糊糊弹。Since we were anything but paper-rich in those days, we had to recycle the bullets we had fired. After each use, we would pick them up from the ground, give them a firm bite to tighten them up and reload them. A few rounds later, we would be firing not the stiff, well-shaped paper bullets that they should be, but saliva-mushed papier mâché pellets!

我的武器库里，有一件"镇库之宝"，是打得最准，手感最好的一把弹弓枪，完全用铁丝缠绕而成，由于用的是粗铁丝（我父亲手劲贼大），刚性极好，哪怕配上粗皮筋，绷得紧紧的，"枪管"部分也不会发生挠曲。The equivalent of a prized Glock in my arsenal was a wire pistol. It turned me into a good shot and had so much oomph in it that just holding it gave me an unspeakable euphoric sensation. The wire used was a thick one (my father had Herculean hands), so the pistol was a sturdy fellah and its 'barrel' had enough rigidity to resist the stress of tough, fully-tensioned elastics. 弹弓枪的靶子分两种：固定靶和移动靶，也就是墙靶和人靶！墙靶好理解：画个靶，挂在墙上或钉在墙上就行了。人靶呢？顾名思义，自然就是两哥们儿互为靶子了！反正弹药是纸折的，不会造成严重伤害，何况朋友们的弹弓枪都不是我父亲做的，准头奇差。可混战中这些"子弹"虽然不长眼，却偏偏喜欢眼睛，经常直奔眼睛而去。The targets for catapult guns came in two types: fixed and moving. Fixed targets were sheets of paper hung on or tacked to the wall with target circles drawn on them. The moving targets? Well, they were friends. Yes, we often practised on each other. 'Practise' is perhaps the wrong word. It was in fact a bit of a free-for-all among a bunch of committed soldiers with the same seriousness as displayed by Sheldon and Co. in a paintball game, the battleground traversed by unguided and misguided missiles in the form of origami ammunition that normally had no chance of hitting the bull's eye in the indiscriminate spray (especially true of those guns not made by my father), but were magically accurate when homing in on the human eye. 那时候,我经常是中弹后眯着充血的兔眼回家的,一看到父母就立刻垂下脑袋,尽量不跟他们对视,怕他们发现……Those days often saw me slinking home with my head down to avoid eye contact with my parents lest they should notice my bloodshot eyes, the red badge of recklessness sustained in the melee...

但做父母的,都是火眼金睛,怎么可能不发现呢? But notice they did, with their enhanced visual acuity that comes with parenthood. 母亲的第一反应就是禁止我再玩这种危险的游戏。她说:"如果眼膜反复受伤,会留下永久性的后遗症,那可是一辈子的事儿。这个道理还用我说吗?" My mother's knee-jerk reaction was to ban me from this dangerous game once and for all. 'You would go blind eventually if your eyes were repeatedly injured like this. You should know better than to bring this upon yourself,' she said, part worried, part annoyed. 我嬉皮笑脸地盯着她看,这是我惯用的伎俩,只要我坚持,她最终会噗嗤一笑,答应我的某个请求。以前百试不爽,但这次不行,她就是不松口。"别以为我会睁一只眼闭一只眼,不行就是不行,"她说。I attempted to cajole her into cutting me some slack with my well-tried ploy: gazing into her eyes while pulling a persistently cheeky, moronic grin, hoping I could outstare her and break her stern countenance, as I had done on numerous occasions before. But it didn't work this time. She was adamant: 'Which part of no don't you understand? If you think I would turn a blind eye to your foolishness, you have another think coming!' 父亲则有点为难:枪是他做的,打枪也是他撺掇的,但儿子老是挂彩,确实也不是个事儿。My father was ambivalent. He was the one who had made the gun in the first place and encouraged his son to join in the fun, but at the end of the day, my getting hurt in the eyes all the time wasn't exactly what he had wanted. 他知道,让我彻底放弃这种游戏吧,我一定失望加失落,于是灵机一动,跟我说:"这样吧,仗就别打了,我给你做一种新靶子,你肯定喜欢。" He knew that I would feel left out if I was coerced into giving up this game. He had a brainwave, which would go some way towards easing my disappointment. He said to me, 'Let's make a deal. You stop fighting with real people and I'll make you a new target, which I'm sure you will like.' 我勉强答应了，心里却直嘀咕：靶子还能变出什么花样来吗？I reluctantly agreed to the deal, but I was incredulous: Targets are targets. How different can a new target be? 可他说到做到，立即动着手制作新靶。父亲信奉"自己动手，丰衣足食"以及勤俭持家的理念，不光动手能力超强，更是废物利用专家，如果他活到今天，一定被奉为绿色生活的楷模。He immediately set about fulfilling his end of the bargain. He was a firm believer of all those proverbs about thrift and self-reliance, like 'A handyman is never a needy man' and 'Waste not, want not'. Besides being adept with his hands, he was also a bit of a hoarder (of junk, in my mother's opinion). On that score, he had sundry idiosyncrasies, which I shall not elaborate. Suffice it to say my father was a recycler of virtuosic calibre. If he were still alive today, he would be hailed as green living incarnate. 他从储藏室一堆井然有序的"垃圾"中找出一个洗得干干净净的空马口铁罐头，朝上的一面已经掀开了一大半，边缘不整齐，他觉得不够好，于是拿出开罐头的小刀（他有一把用了几十年的多功能刀，其中有一片专门用来开罐头，传统的瑞士军刀好像都有这个功能），仔仔细细地把底下那面切了下来，然后把边缘锉滑，在近边缘处打一个小孔，穿进一小截聚氯乙烯塑料绳，挂在院子围墙上。So he whipped out an empty, thoroughly cleaned tin can from a tidy pile of mothballed 'junk' in the utility room. He studied the jagged edge of the top side that had been torn open, and decided it wasn't good enough. He proceeded to cut the bottom disc out with a can opener, which was part of his treasured museum-grade multitool, with utmost care and precision. The disc was then filed down to deburr the edge and a hole was made near the edge. He threaded a length of PVC string through the hole and hung the metal disc on the wall of our yard.

他说："依看，格个圆片本来就有几个同心圆，伊格用场是增强材料格刚性,更加耐压,因为罐头里面是负压,但用料勿用增加。依讲,像不像靶环?依以前练习格靶子,画在纸上,特大,现在依打得更加准了,可以用更小格靶子了。"He explained, 'If you look at the tin disc, you can see it comes with some concentric circles. They are designed to make the disc stronger against pressure that is generated by the vacuum inside the can, without using more metal. But they look like target circles, don't they? You have been practising on large targets drawn on paper. Now that you are better at it, you can move on to a smaller one.' 他还告诉我,本想让我把子弹在图章印泥上按一下再打出去,这样可以在靶子上留下印记,但考虑到我还不是神枪手,子弹乱飞的结果是:墙上血染的风采很难看,我手上的彩绘很难看,我母亲涨红的脸色也一定很难看,于是他速速打消了这个念头。He also told me that he had initially toyed with the idea of sweetening the deal by inking my paper bullets so any hit would leave a red mark on the target, but had swiftly banished that thought because of his reservations about my marksmanship. It would have left my hands in a rouged mess, added a cryptically modernistic rosy mural to the wall and rendered my mother's face crimson with exasperation. 他对我的枪法不放心,我完全理解,因为他挂马口铁靶子时,让我当他的下手,为了提高我的操锤技能,他自己扶着大铁钉,让我用榔头把钉子敲进墙壁,我自信满满,毫不手软,"啪啪"两记——全砸在父亲捏着铁钉的手指上了!他吹了吹发紫的拇指,困惑地打量我:"我弄勿懂,侬瞄准格是钉头,是伐?格么哪能对我格手指头瞄得介准呢?"I fully understood my father's reservations. When he was hanging up the tin target, he beckoned me over to give him a hand. Treating me as an apprentice whose tinkering skills needed improving, he asked me to try hammering the nail into the wall while he held it in place with his thumb and forefinger. That's exactly what I did, except I missed the nail and hit his thumb both times I slammed the hammer down with the surety of a pro. While blowing at his bruised thumb, he gave me a quizzical look: 'You were aiming at the nail, were you not? But the hammer had a mind of its own?'

为了弥补无法留下视觉标记的缺憾，他在我的弹弓枪上加装了一条皮筋，增加了射程，这样我可以站得更远一点，马口铁靶子就显得更小一点，只要打到，就相当于中了十环，而且会发出"当"的一声脆响，煞是好听，让射手很有成就感！Seeing that painting the target with every hit wasn't an option, my father added a rubber band to the pistol to extend the range, allowing me to stand farther away from the target, which would in turn look smaller. Any hit on any part of the target would be as good as scoring a bullseye, not to mention the added bonus of a delightful ding that could be considered a salvo to bolster the shooter's ego.

一把精品级弹弓枪、一个叮当作响的靶子，让我着迷了很长时间。我天天对着那个靶子潜心练习"枪法"，到后来弹无虚发，"哨哨"声不绝。有天小鹤的弟弟"老四"（大名吴元俊）来找我玩，我自然不会错过一展身手的好机会，装上纸弹后，没有瞄准，抬手便是一枪，"哨！"居然打中了！我自知纯属侥幸，但还是沾沾自喜，老四则看得目瞪口呆。The combination of this premium-quality catapult pistol and the ding-dong target proved to be more than a five-minute wonder for me. Practising on that target became my daily routine and I got to a point where every shot I fired would score, and score with that metallic report. Xiao He has a younger brother, WU Yuanjun. We called him Lao Si, meaning Number Four. He was the fourth sibling of their all-boy family. One day, Number Four came to visit. I had to show off to him what an ace shot I had become. I loaded the paper bullet and casually pointed the pistol, held at the waist level, in the general direction of the target. A stab in the dark indeed. I pulled the trigger. Ding! 'T was a hit! My beaming visage didn't betray my knowledge of the fact that it was a fluke. Needless to say, the monumental feat left Number Four gobsmacked. And me, smug-faced.

弹弓　The Hand Catapult

所以说,用自制的弹弓打墙靶,我实在提不起兴趣。何况,谁都知道,弹弓跟弹弓枪是有区别的,后者虽然多了一个"枪"字,但它只是玩具,没有一点儿实用价值,但少了一个"枪"字的弹弓,可是正儿八经的武器。That's why I found the idea of using my DIY catapult against some artificial target unappetising. Moreover, it is common knowledge that a catapult pistol is just a toy, despite the ominous presence of a firearm in its name, whereas the innocuous-sounding hand catapult is a *bona fide* weapon. 这,就是前面提到的"猎鸟行动"的缘起。And the above is an overture to *Operation Birding* mentioned earlier.

我要试试新武器的实战效用,首先想到的是我们家屋顶的常客:麻雀。I needed a live target to shoot at, to find out how my new weapon would fare in the real world. Sparrows! Yes, they were the first to leap to mind, as our roof was their haunt. 我招呼黑狮和小黄过来观战,黑狮很听话,在屋前坐定,小黄爱理不理,甚至懒得猜一猜我想干吗,我不断发出"吱吱"声,吸引他的注意力,让他别走开。I summoned Leonoir and Gingerlet. They would be my audience. Leonoir was his usual obsequious self, ready to do my bidding no matter what. He seated himself in front of the house, no questions asked. Gingerlet couldn't care less and he certainly made no secret of it. He didn't even bother to venture a guess. I had to keep making a special sound with my mouth to attract his attention. This noise is apparently unique to China, or so I thought. People speaking different dialects in different parts of China seem to rely on the same sonic note for communication with the cat population. I had used it on cats of different breeds in foreign lands (so I could pet them or take a picture of them, for example) to no avail, so I came to the conclusion that this noise, produced by sucking air in through the interdental gaps, i.e. the only vents in the oral gate constructed with upper incisors biting the lower lip, the audible vibration being modulated by the opening and closing of the upper lip, was the single-phoneme *lingua franca* for human-to-feline communication that ought to be acknowledged as part of the Chinese language. (A quick survey among my friends on Wechat indicates that this conclusion of mine couldn't be further from the truth. Oh, well, I do get ahead of myself sometimes.) 我伸出弹弓给他们嗅，不明就里的黑狮摇着尾巴赞颂有加："主人啊，你真厉害，我不知道这是干啥用的，反正……你就是厉害。我就等着看好戏啦！"小黄嗅了嗅，知道这玩意儿不好吃，别过脸去，但他并没有完全不给面子，还像模像样地眯眼沉吟片刻，似乎是想整明白，主人的葫芦里到底卖的是啥药。I let them sniff the catapult. The highly impressionable Leonoir showered me with excessive tail-signalled praises: 'You are awesome, Master! I haven't the foggiest idea what this is for, but you are awesome just the same! I wouldn't miss the show for the world.' Gingerlet gave it a half-hearted peck and turned his head away. He knew this was not something edible, at least not for a cat. But there was no discernible sign of disdain in his body language. In fact, he looked pensive with a classic feline squint: Hmm, I wonder what Master is up to this time!

  我抬头看了看屋顶，只见一只麻雀栖息在屋檐上。I looked up at the roof of our house. A sparrow perched on the eaves. 那个年代，兴化普通房子的天花板一般都是三米高，那么屋檐离地应该不足三米，我当时的身高，保守估计也有160厘米了，拉弹弓时，右手（我抓筷子、抓笔用的是右手，但其他场合好像是左撇子，例如拉弹弓用左手，抛飞碟用左手，单手玩杂耍也用左手，所以握弹弓的手是右手）略高于头部。再加上我跟墙壁之间的距离，我右手跟麻雀的距离，应该是两米多一点。In those days, an ordinary house in Xinghua would typically have a ceiling height of just over three yards, so the eaves would be a little lower than that. I was at least 5 foot 3 at the time. When I drew the loaded leather pocket back with my left hand (which is the dominant hand when I'm not holding a pen or chopsticks) while steadying the frame with my right hand (which is the off hand unless I'm eating or writing), my right hand would be a little higher than my head. When the distance between where I stood and the wall is factored in, my right hand would be just over two yards from the little bird poised on the tip of a rafter. 写到这里，我起身对着房间天花板的某一点比划了一下，然后用卷尺一量，我记忆中当时右手距麻雀，大概就是230厘米左右。这是非常近的距离，如果是开枪打靶，新手也应该百发百中了。Just now, I stopped writing to take some measurements. I held my right hand above my head and gauged the distance between that hand and a chosen spot on the ceiling. I found a distance that matched my memory. I then measured it: 7 feet 6 inches. Even a rookie would not have missed the target at this point-blank range.

　　我记得那只麻雀扭动脖子一会儿看看我，一会儿看看我的两个伙伴，似乎未起疑心，也不惊恐。它也许每天都在这个屋檐午休，看惯了我们一家人，包括一猫一狗，从来都是井水不犯河水，从未心生恐惧。而在我眼里，麻雀们长得都差不多，分不清是张三李四赵五王六，更何况在做弹弓前，我从未关注过这些屋"檐客"。I remember seeing the sparrow rubbernecking between me and my two buddies. It didn't seem to grow suspicious of my intention, nor did it look fearful. It might have been a resident of this part of the roof for a long time and become accustomed to seeing members of my family, including the two four-legged creatures, going about our business each day. No line had ever been crossed. The sparrow and my family had, until this point, lived in parallel universes separated by, as it were, an invisible hedge over which occasional, dispassionate peeks might be exchanged. What was there to fear? And to me, sparrows all looked the same. I couldn't tell who was Tom, who was Dick and who was Harry. In fact, before I made my catapult, I had not even shown a passing interest in any of these passers-by.

　　（由于工作繁忙，有一个多星期未写一字，今天回家的路上，有只麻雀飞到我近旁，在我脚边蹦蹦跳跳，还几度斜着脑袋瞅瞅我，似乎在

Leonoir and Gingerlet 伙伴行

提醒我:"喂,你那麻雀故事,怎么戛然而止啦? 我和我的小伙伴们都在等着下文呢!"好吧,我接着写。Work has been hectic of late. An action-packed week or so meant I had to put the writing on hold for as long. On my way home today, a sparrow landed near me and hopped round my feet. It cocked its head to one side and eyed me up and down. I think it was asking me, 'What's happened to your sparrow story? Me and my friends are all waiting for the other shoe to drop, you know!' Alright then, I shall oblige.)

就在我瞄准那只麻雀时,它把目光转向了我,看着我。Just as I was taking aim with the catapult, my target turned towards me and started studying me. 距离这么近,我能清楚地看到他的小眼睛,绿豆般大小,贼亮贼亮的,它只知道我一反常态在观察它,但不知道我想干嘛,更不可能明白它即将大祸临头,小命难保。Being so close to the sparrow, I was able to see its tiny beady eye, which seemed to be saying to me, 'I know you are watching me, for a change, but I don't know why.' That's right, it did not know for what reason I was watching it, much less that fatality was about to be visited upon its life, taking the light out of its tiny beady eyes.

就在那个瞬间,另一只麻雀闯进了我的脑海。At that precise moment, another sparrow, or my memory of it, gatecrashed this hunting game, in a manner of speaking. 那是好几年前,我们家还在兴化戴南乡下时,村里一位叔叔送给我一只小麻雀,他在谷仓里找到了两个雀仔,我和他儿子,一人一个。That sparrow was a baby one, given to me by a villager when we were living in Dainan Commune, several years back. He had found a couple of hatchlings in his barn. He had kept one for his son and given the other to me as a present. 我母亲找来一根细麻绳,让我拴住麻雀的一只脚,让它飞不远。I tied one of its feet with a hemp string that my mother gave me. It worked as a leash. 我负责喂米饭给它吃,还得保护它,不让附近的猫狗把它给吃了。My task as its custodian was twofold: to keep it fed, with cooked rice, and to keep it safe, from prowling cats and hungry dogs in the neighbourhood. 起初我很兴奋,因为有了个小伙伴,但我很快发现,这位小伙伴并不乐意跟我混,它一心想飞走。Initially, I was very excited to have this little companion, but it didn't take me long to realise that my joy was not reciprocated: The sparrow chick was merely a reluctant captive whose sole interest was not in my friendship, but in getting out of it.

当天傍晚,我从外面回家时,手里只有那根麻绳,麻雀却不见了。母亲问:"咦,麻雀呢?"我说:"放了。它妈妈肯定在找它。"At dusk, I came home with the string in my hand, but the sparrow was nowhere to be seen. Mother asked what I had done to the sparrow. I replied, 'I set it free. I'm sure its mum was looking for it.'(我知道我当时说了大意如此的话,但具体怎么说的,不记得了,原话是我母亲告诉我的。I knew I had said something to that effect at the time, but couldn't remember exactly how I had said it. Luckily, the answer was just a phone call away. On the other end of the line was, of course, my mother.)

当年那个雀仔绝望忧郁的眼神,跟我现在瞄准的这只麻雀毫无戒备的眼神,足以让我放下了弹弓。打麻雀的故事就这样草草收场,无果而终。In the flashback, I saw sadness and despair in the eyes of that baby sparrow; in reality, the bird I was about to shoot down was gazing at me, all trusting and defenceless. That was enough to disarm the armed catapult and put paid to the tentative sniper's fiendish agenda. I lowered my weapon. An attempted murder was thus aborted, in an anticlimax.

小黄本来就是稀里糊涂地被拉来观战的,等了一会儿发现没啥名堂,一头雾水地走开了;黑狮是知情者,等着给我喝彩,但看我迟迟下不了手,觉得挺没劲的,也走开了。后来我才知道,他是到屋后跟青蛙玩儿去了。Gingerlet hadn't quite cottoned on to what I was doing in the first place. He waited for a bit. Seeing nothing exciting was going on, he walked away, none the wiser. Leonoir had figured out my intention and was ready to hail my exploit, until he witnessed his master succumbing to a pang of compunction. Underwhelmed, he also walked away (to play with frogs, now we know). 我心有不甘，于是绕到屋后，看看还有没有其他活靶子让我试试新武器的威力。I wasn't ready to give up just yet. I ambled along to the untamed nature behind the house in search of some other live targets with which to initiate my new sidearm.

大鸟的故事　The Big Bird

兴化离盐城不远，直线距离大概 50 公里。Xinghua is about 30 miles, as the crow flies, from another town called Yancheng. 盐城以滩涂湿地著称，而湿地是涉禽的天堂。中国最美、最有名的涉禽要数丹顶鹤，也就是美术作品里的"仙鹤"（所谓的"鹤寿"真实不虚，有的丹顶鹤确实能活到 70 岁）。盐城湿地正是丹顶鹤这种鸟中王族的冬季行宫。

丹顶鹤。Red-crowned crane.

Leonoir and Gingerlet 伙伴行

Yancheng, meaning Salt City, is so named because of the salinity of its soil, as its territory covers vast swathes of tidal flats on the coast of the East China Sea. As we know, wetlands are home to wading birds. In China, the best known stunners among them are the red-crowned cranes, their fame built upon their sublime grace and the publicity they receive through Chinese paintings that feature them as a symbol of luck and longevity. They are also known as Immortal Cranes, mainly because they can live up to 70 years. The marshy areas in Yancheng are a perfect winter habitat for this species of avian nobility.

既然兴化是盐城的近邻，那么时不时飞来一些丹顶鹤，也就不足为奇了。它们喜水，对人类没有太大兴趣，因此它们时常盘桓在我家屋后那片僻静的鱼塘区，也就是黑狮跟青蛙捉迷藏的那一带。The proximity of Xinghua to Yancheng by a 'crow's flight' also means high accessibility for these cranes, who are excellent aviators in their own right. They are more interested in water than in humans and that's why the fish pond-studded 'outback' behind our house, devoid of human presence, became their haunt. 'Haunt' may be an overstatement, but if the season was right, one could easily spot them round where Leonoir played hide-and-seek with frogs. 确实，就人类居住环境而言，"屋后"与"屋前"的意象形成对照。屋前的空间，是被人们调伏、规整化的格局；屋后，则是放肆、自由，并因此生机盎然的"自然"。我家的"屋后"，就是一道鱼鸟相伴亦相忘的"江湖"风景。Come to think of it, at the conceptual level, the view in front of a human abode is very different from that behind it: What it gives on to in the front is an enclave of nature tamed and disciplined, reconfigured to suit the inhabitant's practical or aesthetic predilections; behind the residential structure, on the other hand, is nature unspoilt and unbridled, teeming with life that is free and with a riot of expressions thereof - a sanctuary whose sanctity remains intact. The area behind our house was, for example, a water world, home to both fish and fowl, each to their own and each in company with the other.

我那天在屋后看到了三只丹顶鹤，离我最近的那只在二十米开外。That day, I saw three 'Immortal Cranes' there and one of them was only 20 yards or so from where I was standing. 上个世纪八十年代末，江苏人大概都听说过一位年轻的丹顶鹤保育员，为保护小天鹅而牺牲的事迹。那个故事感人至深、催人泪下。这位保育员叫徐秀娟①，想了解她的生平和事迹的，可以在网上搜到她的资料。In the late 1980s, many people in Jiangsu would have heard how a young conservation worker, XU Xiujuan, had given her life to the breeding of endangered or rare bird species, including red-crowned cranes, and had given up her life to save the lives of baby swans. The story is as inspiring as it is heartbreaking. See footnote for her bio. 但当时这件事还没发生，我还没有被感化呢。But that incident happened many years after the 'animal test' I was trying to conduct with my catapult, so my innate soft spot for animals had not been further softened by that story yet. 不知为何，大多数男孩子或多或少都有一点残酷，嵌在他的天性里。I don't know why, but it seems that most boys have a cruel streak in their nature. It's just less pronounced in some than in others. 例如我在家里负责剥毛豆，经常有一些豆虫从豆荚里爬出来，我如果有时间，就会把这些豆虫放在蚂蚁窝附近，观察蚂蚁如何百折不挠、视死如归地跟比自己大几十倍的豆虫搏斗，豆虫最后精疲力尽，任由蚂蚁拖进蚂蚁窝。For example, in my family, I was the one responsible for podding fresh soybeans. Every now and then, a worm would crawl out of the pod. If I had time on my hand, I would place the worm near an anthill and watch the ants wrestle the worm, many, many times their size, into submission and eventually

---

① *XU Xiujuan (1964—1987), daughter of an underprivileged crane-breeding Manchurian family in Northeast China, helped her parents feed and tend crane chicks from a young age and decided to make it her lifelong career. At age 22, as an expert breeder with an impeccable track record, she was invited by Yancheng Nature Reserve to work on a crane conservation project. She brought with her three swan eggs, all of which hatched successfully. A year later, two of the swans lost their way in the reed marshes. She spent days looking for them and later drowned in the river, exhausted and grief-stricken. A statue was put up in her memory inside Yancheng Nature Reserve.*

drag the knackered worm into the anthill. Every battle was epic testimony to the legendary valiance and tenacity of the formidable formic warriors. 我能津津有味地观战两小时，一路为蚁兵加油！仔细想想，这就是一种残忍，从生命的毁灭中获取快感。I was a loyal spectator, generously spending up to two hours watching the action with rapt attention and cheering the ant soldiers on. Let's face it, that was cruelty, plain and simple, wasn't it? Getting high from watching the termination of a life.

　　机会难得，我立即拉开弹弓，瞄准那只丹顶鹤的翅膀，刚才不忍心打下小鸟，我现在也不可能对这只大鸟真的下毒手，所以只是瞄准了它的翅膀。I saw my chance and armed my catapult. I took aim at the crane's wing, not its head. Since I hadn't taken that easy and potentially deadly shot at the little sparrow earlier, I wasn't going to cause serious damage to this beautiful giant now. 它向前迈了几步，我屏住呼吸，闭起左眼，三点一线紧紧咬住它的翅膀，我的心吊到了嗓子眼……然后，在眩晕的刹那，左手一松……The crane took a few steps forward. Heart racing like mad, I trained the catapult on its wing while holding my breath. The momentary deprivation of oxygen made my chest tight and gave me a slight head rush... Then I released the shot… "啪！"弹丸果然击中了丹顶鹤的翅膀，但我能感觉到，那么小的弹丸疲弱地打在它健硕的翅膀上，简直就像把一片树叶扔进河里，恐怕涟漪都无法激起。With a muted thud, I scored. The shot hit the wing. But the projectile was so small and its impact so weak against the thick feathered armour that a leaf gliding into a river might have caused a bigger splash. 它愣了一下，慢慢扭头看了我一眼，似乎不确定到底发生了什么。"是我的错觉呢，还是真的有个东西碰了我一下呢？咦，那里站着一个瘦猴儿，看着我，手里拿着不知是什么东西，恐怕不怀好意。我还是小心为妙吧，走也！"它张开巨大的翅膀，扑腾两下，拔地而起，飞走了。The crane stopped whatever it was doing. Slowly, it scanned its environment, until it saw me. It looked mystified. 'What was that? Did something touch me? Or was I imagining it? Oh, there's a skinny specimen of *homo erec-*

tus over there staring at me. He looks a bit creepy. I cannot tell what he is holding in his hand. Better safe than sorry. Off I go!' The wary bird unfurled its huge wings, flapped them, heaved itself off the ground and flew away.

我的"猎鸟行动"就这样以失败告终了。It was on that note that *Operation Birding* came to an end. Mission scuppered. 两只鸟，一小一大，小鸟对我的恃武视而不见，大鸟对我的动武不屑一顾，最终的结果是：志得意满出门，垂头丧气回家。Two birds, one small and one large, both roundly ignored me. One didn't even recognise the threat of force from me; the other decided not to entertain my use of force. I had gone on the expedition a cocky would-be hunter; I returned, a crestfallen might-have-been.

Leonoir and Gingerlet　伙伴行

郭逗和插刀　　The Sisters

说起鸟类,说起垂"头",让我想起跟另外两只禽类动物的缘分,其中之一就是头上的"凤冠"长得很美很别致的"角头",吴方言念"郭逗"。Speaking of 'crest', in the general context of birds, I am reminded of *Gwodou* (Horned Head, pronounced *jiaotou* in Putonghua and *Gwodou* in the Greater Shanghai dialect; renamed Godot hereinafter), one of two avian friends I had some years back, so named because she had a very striking crest. 另外一只叫"插刀",她们是我们家下放在戴南时养的"下蛋"鸡。The other one was *Chadao*, or Swordsman. They were both hens and we kept them when we were living in that village in Dainan as 'cadres sent down to the countryside for reeducation by the peasants'. There was an unspoken pact between the hens and their owners: We fed them; they repaid us with eggs. 插刀的名字也来自她的体貌特征:她小时候骨瘦如柴,毛发稀疏,以至于翅肘儿支楞着,在背部凸起,就像插了两把刀一样,有点畸形,走路也挺别扭的。长大后好多了,"插刀"也不明显了,但我们保留了她的雅号。The name Swordsman (I know it should be Swordswoman, but hey, let's not get too pedantic) also came from her physical feature. When Swordsman was a baby, she was a bag of skin and bone, clad in a coat of flimsy down and woefully scanty feathers, with two bald wings pitiably sticking up like a pair of sheathed blades. That and her awkward gait made her look somewhat deformed. When she matured, however, she became more 'normal' and the edged weapons became less conspicuous, but I didn't change her name. 郭逗就不同了,她发育正常,体态敦实,步态从容。Godot was the opposite. She was the picture of health as a chick and grew up to be the proverbial hen, with a wide body and a steady waddle.

郭逗和插刀,生的蛋数量差不多,但颜色不同,郭逗的蛋是红褐色的，很厚实，有次我没握牢，掉在地上，不仅没碎，连裂纹都没有。插刀的蛋跟她的毛色一样，呈淡黄色，蛋壳比较薄，容易破。Godot and Swordsman were equally prolific in laying eggs, but their eggs were of different colours. Godot gave us solid reddish brown eggs whereas Swordsman's were a pale yellow, the colour of her feathers, and more fragile. One day, one of Godot's eggs fell from my hand and landed on the floor, but it did not so much as show a single hairline crack. 对她们生的鸡蛋，我非常熟悉，因为从鸡窝里取鸡蛋是由我负责的，那是一件美差，一场不会失望的等待。I am familiar with the physical properties of their eggs because fetching eggs from the coop was my job, and a very pleasant one at that. Pleasant, because the job involved a wait that was in-

郭逗和插刀。Godot and Swordsman.

variably rewarded with that which was waited for. 每次看见郭逗或插刀大白天进了鸡窝，我就会早早地守候在鸡窝外面，手里捏着一把米，有时一等就是十几、二十分钟，等她们一出来，我就把米撒在她们面前，犒劳她们下蛋有功。 The wait would begin when I saw Godot or Swordsman ducking into their coop in daytime, and would last up to 20 minutes. I always had a handful of rice at the ready, so they could have a well-deserved treat when they came out.

郭逗和插刀是好朋友，成天一起觅食，形影不离。 Godot and Swordsman were the best of friends, like two peas in a pod. They foraged and hunted together, an activity that took up most, if not all, of their waking moments. One would not be seen without the other. 郭逗更加剽悍一点，见到大蜈蚣总是先冲上去跟它搏斗，插刀则在一旁助威，瞅见机会就上前啄几口，战胜蜈蚣后，姐妹俩分而啖之，很少争抢。 Godot was the more butch of the two. When confronted with a large centipede, for instance, Godot would be the one to launch herself into the battle and unleash the full force of her aggression on the poor soul while Swordsman lent moral support from the sidelines and stole a peck or two whenever it was safe to do so. After the centipede was overpowered, they would partake of the viand in an uncommon spirit of sharing, with no sign of sibling rivalry of the pecking and clawing type.

说鸡"成天"觅食，一点都不过分，它们确实日出而作，日入而息，一天到晚不是在吃东西就是在找东西吃。 I don't think I can be accused of exaggeration when I say chickens spend practically all their life ingesting or seeking sustenance. It is actually very true. From sunup to sundown, they are always there busying themselves with one task and one task only: eating something or looking for something to eat. 我就利用郭逗和插刀的这个特点，捉弄她们。 If one can call it a weakness, then that's the weakness I exploited, for my own amusement. 夏天天黑得晚，我们吃晚饭时，她们还没回窝，我左手端着饭碗，右手拿着筷子，在屋子外面站着或蹲着，郭逗和插刀就赶紧过来，等候施舍。 In summer, it was still light at supper time, too early for Godot and Swordsman to call it a day and retire for the night. I would be standing or squatting outside our house, a bowl in my left hand and a pair of chopsticks in my right. Godot and Swordsman would come running. They would not so much mob me as hang round me. They knew they were in for a treat… in the form of scraps of food that I would casually dole out. 我们的晚饭一般是泡饭，就是中午的剩饭，加水，佐以两种小菜，其中一种是咸菜，例如萝卜干，另一种可能是熟菜，例如红烧豇豆。嘿，又是红烧豇豆，前面在讲述黑狮吃咸鸭蛋的故事时就提到过，这里再次提起，显然我确实很喜欢这道菜，在脑海里挥之不去。It was slim pickings on our summer dinner menu: *paofan*, or 'waterlogged' steamed rice; a couple of savouries more like *hors d'oeuvres* than proper dishes. The *paofan* was basically leftover steamed rice swimming in cold boiled water. It was soggy and bland (but not unpalatable thanks to the unique texture and fragrance of rice), so we needed something salty to go with it. The savouries usually included a cold relish, like a cucumber or radish pickle or a salted duck egg, and a cooked vegetable dish, like braised cowpeas. I am sure we had many other cooked vegetables, but this particular dish was my number one favourite. That's why it sticks in my mind.

　　郭逗和插刀守住我的左右两翼后，我就故意慢条斯理地用筷子从碗里捞起几颗米粒，延长她们期盼的时间，然后忽远忽近地抛给她们，她们就奔跑着，在或远或近的地方啄食这些米粒。Now that I was flanked by Godot and Swordsman, I would fish out a few pieces of rice with chopsticks. I would do so with deliberate hesitation to prolong the tantalisation, before flicking the rice in a random direction. They would rush to the landing point to pick up the rice and the distance they needed to cover depended on the range of my throw. 在这种短跑比赛中，郭逗的优势很明显，插刀则徒有虚名。In a race like this, Godot had a clear edge over Swordsman, who couldn't do justice to her name. 等到我希望插刀也能吃上一口时，就把米粒抛到插刀身后，让插刀捷足先登。

When I decided it was Swordsman's turn to be fed, I would make sure the rice landed behind Swordsman, to give her a head start.

像这样喂了几个回合后,我再次捞起几粒米,再次将筷子举到一定的高度,既让郭逗和插刀看得清清楚楚(不知鸡是否也有唾液,如果有的话,她们此时一定在猛咽口水),又让她们觉得这些米粒唾手可得。然后,我的筷子头一松,米粒又落回碗里!After a few rounds of feeding like this, I once again scooped up a few grains of rice and once again raised my chopsticks high enough for Godot and Swordsman to see the rice and salivate over it, if salivation is something chickens do too, and low enough to create the low-hanging fruit effect. Then, I decoupled the chopsticks. The rice fell back into the bowl.

郭逗和插刀一路狂奔,冲到碗的正下方,在我面前紧张地寻找掉下来的米粒,遍寻不得,抬头看看我的碗,低头继续找,当然还是找不到,我就得意地看着她们,心想:"怎么样?小脑袋不够用了吧?米粒根本没落地,你怎么可能找到呢?太盲目了,真是'鸡盲'!"Right on cue, Godot and Swordsman scurried to the spot below the bowl. (If they could fly, they would.) They frantically searched for the rice that was supposed to have fallen to the ground, but they couldn't see any. They looked up at the bowl to make sure that it was the right spot and then carried on searching, again in vain. Their bemused look gave me a mildly pleasant sensation of *schadenfreude*: 'Blind as a bat, no, blind as a chicken, you two! The rice was caught by the bowl, but you didn't see it, did you? And you can't figure out why, can you, with your tiny brains?' 我就这样逗她们玩,几个回合后不忍心再欺负她们了,再让米粒落地,让她们吃个痛快。I would tease them like this until I started feeling more sorry for them than amused. I would then give them a generous helping to thank them for humouring my mischief.

鸡拳秘笈　Hen-Style Kungfu

很多年后，我才明白，在那种特定的觅食条件下，以最快的速度找到并抢到食物，郭逗和插刀靠的是条件反射，不是靠深思熟虑的计策，她们的举动是不经大脑的，脑袋再大、再聪明，也来不及看清楚了再行动。如果看清楚了、想明白了再决定是否冲过去，也许可以避免盲目性，但获得食物的机会也就错失了。所以在那一刻，最佳选择是先冲过去再说。It wasn't until many, many years later that I realised Godot and Swordsman were acting, not by some well-thought-out stratagem, but on reflex, in order to find the food in the shortest time possible and beat their rival to it. It would have been too slow if they had gone through a 'thinking' process, so a larger, intellectually superior brain would not have helped. In fact, in a situation like this, if you spent too long observing and weighing your odds, you might be able to avoid looking stupid, but you would certainly miss the opportunity. It's a tradeoff between (a) conserving energy by staying put and (b) getting there first in the hope of accessing more energy. Given the circumstances, your best bet would be the latter. 以武术技击为例。记得一位师父说过，高手的较量，其实就是逼对方失误，或者说，最终胜败取决于谁先失误。Take for example close combat in the context of martial arts (boxing included). A *sifu* told me once that a high-level showdown is in essence a process of forcing a mistake out of the opponent while trying not to be the first one to err. 所以对抗时，一般都有佯攻动作，诱敌深入，自己则以逸待劳，趁对方像郭逗、插刀那样盲目突入之机，后发制人。For this reason, confrontation often features feints and deceptive moves to lure the opponent into a trap. You have a counterstrike up your sleeve ready for him and you pray that he would, like Godot and Swordsman, rush headlong (and headlessly) into your snare where he would be greeted with a telling blow or two.

Leonoir and Gingerlet 伙伴行

当然这是事后分解和分析的经验谈,现场的一切都是在电光石火的瞬间发生的,全靠训练出来的自然反应,抽象的理性思考毫无用处。That's all very well, but the real world is built with real brick and mortar and does not operate on *a posteriori* deconstruction and analysis. In this real world, trained reflexes are more serviceable than high IQ and abstract reasoning has no place when the outcome hinges on a split-second decision. 十八年前我开始练习咏春拳,慢慢体会到,咏春拳妙就妙在于它发扬了郭逗和插刀的精神:看到机会,先扑上去再说。而咏春拳的高桩灵动、中线原理和短距缠打的战术,决定了拳手不怕对方放空,对方虚晃一招时,正好提供了突破的机会。I started dabbling in Wing Chun(Yongchunquan)18 years ago. I quickly learnt that the instinct of Godot and Swordsman, which I had considered dumb, was actually central to the Wing Chun combat philosophy: 'You see a chance, you go for it, now!' This may indeed be unwise in the eyes of some other forms of martial arts, but in the realm of Wing Chun, the opponent's deliberate deception may render himself vulnerable and such vulnerability can be exploited with Wing Chun's high horse-stand (for greater responsiveness and manoeuvrability), its centre-line principle, its close-range trapping and 'stickiness' and its elbow-powered, short-travel punches.

写到这里,抬头一看,天哪,我这一段跑题跑到天边去了!不好意思,这就勒缰兜回来吧。Goodness me! I was totally lost in my reverie and what was supposed to be a brief deviation has ended up teleporting us to another universe. *Mea culpa*. Let me rein in this daydreaming mustang and circle back to the subject...

兜回来,回到哪里?哦,郭逗和插刀!Back to the subject of what? Oh, of Godot and Swordsman. 现在想起来了,我想说,本以为自己很聪明,以戏弄二鸡为乐,其实郭逗和插刀用行动告诉我:"有机会就得试一试,哪怕出丑!"I meant to say, now I remember, that in those days, I thought I was being clever tantalising the chickens with a cliffhanger followed by a plummeting letdown, but that wasn't clever at all. Godot and

Swordsman followed a simple philosophy, that chances are to be grabbed in the moment and not to be wasted just so you don't make a fool of yourself.

Leonoir and Gingerlet 伙伴行

双姝戏蛇　　The Duel

兴化是著名的水乡，最常见的蛇就是水蛇，我作为小学生参加农业劳动时，其中有一项农活就是在水稻田里拔除杂草，拔着拔着，就有水蛇拦在面前，其实不是故意拦路，它怕人，担心逃不掉，所以诈死，我不敢惊动它，只能屏住呼吸从它上方悄悄跨过去，过一会儿回头一看，它已经消失了。Xinghua is known as the Land of Water（an oxymoron in English, but the literal meaning of *shuixiang* is 'home place of water'）and the most common reptile of the *slithering* type there is the water snake. When I was a primary school pupil, we used to work in the fields as part of our extramural programme. One of the common farming activities we were allowed to take part in, because it required no training, was weeding the rice fields. It involved pulling up weeds from the waterlogged paddy with our hands. Sometimes I would see a snake lying ahead, motionless. It was not a dead snake, I knew. It was a spooked snake that was playing possum. I would hold my breath, gingerly step over it and carry on weeding. A few seconds later, I would turn round to spy on it, and it would be gone. 戴南农村，水蛇就更多了，我们家屋里屋外经常见到它们，有时早上起来，挪动桶形圆凳，就会看到一条小蛇钻出来，嗖的一声夺门而逃，它可能是来我们家取暖的。冷血动物嘛，天气一转凉就难以保持体温了。Water snakes were more common in the rural part of Dainan. They would be seen inside and about our house. One of them might suddenly appear from underneath a piece of furniture in the morning and quickly make its way out before getting squashed. We would know that it had spent the night in the house to keep its cold-blooded body warm.

郭逗可能想开开荤，有次居然主动挑衅一条小水蛇，她拉上插刀，摆开1-1阵形，让插刀闷头猛啄蛇尾，自己则疯狂袭击蛇头，羽毛竖直、凤冠紫红，嘴里还发出"郭郭"之声为自己壮胆。寡不敌众的蛇拼命挣扎，使出浑身解数，"蛇行"、"鞭尾"、"昂首"、"张牙"、"吐信"，负隅顽抗，场面极为惨烈。One day, Godot decided to take on a small snake. Perhaps she wanted to try it for taste. She marshalled Swordsman and herself into a 1-1 formation. Swordsman was to pin down the tail of the snake with swift, relentless pecking and she did so in silence and with full dedication. Godot herself frantically struck the snake's head while clucking, and the clucking emboldened herself to attack even harder. Her feathers stood up and her crest turned purple. The grievously outnumbered snake put up a desperate fight. It pulled out all the stops and pulled out all the tricks in the serpentine duelling repertoire: slithering, tail whipping, head rearing, snarling and hissing. It was a savage battle of blood and sand. 最终的战果是：小蛇遍体鳞伤，成功逃脱，不知所终；两只鸡浑身是血，一地鸡毛，悻悻而归。The campaign ended in a draw: After losing a lot of blood, the snake slipped away to nurse its badly mauled body. After losing a lot of feathers, the two chickens were left staring at each other's gory bodies. The reptile never repeated the mistake of venturing out of the woods into this neck of the woods; the fowl limped home, in a mood so foul.

Leonoir and Gingerlet 伙伴行

矢记 Foul Play

既然回忆起一桩桩"鸡事",如果不讲"鸡屎"的故事,那就太对不起我的读者了。Now that we are on the topic of 'fowl play', it would be grossly remiss of me - and a sorry loss for the reader - not to tell you about my experiment with the 'foul'.

那年我四岁半,在崇明的生活快结束了。I was four and a half, shortly before I was to leave Chongming. 有一天我在院子里正当中看到一滩新鲜的鸡屎,淡棕色,透着一点橙色,边缘齐整,状如传统的杏元饼干。One day, I saw a tidy wad of fresh chicken droppings in the middle of the yard. It was a bronze colour brightened with a glistening shade of amber. How shall I describe its shape? Well, it looked like the top half of a macaroon. 显然,有这么一只鸡,醒来后走出鸡窝,伸伸脖子,拍拍翅膀,吐故纳新,就地方便,给大地奉献这一抔肥沃的"心意"。Obviously it was a fertile gift to Mother Earth from a refreshed chicken out of its coop in celebration of a fine morning, after its rise-and-shine routine of neck craning, wing flapping and deep clucky breathing.

溏心蛋。*A soft-boiled egg.*

- 139 -

鸡屎尚未凝固,还处于半流质状态,但表面已经有一层薄膜,这种鸡屎的"学名"好像叫溏鸡屎,其质地很像溏心鸡蛋。

我知道,这时我要是用手指碰一下这种"心很软",一定会戳破表层,沾上鸡屎,我就会成为堂姐表姐们的笑柄,那可万万使不得！The solid waste wasn't solid yet. It was still quite runny. I could see a thin film forming on the top. I don't know if there's a Latin nomenclature for this type of excrement, but 'gooey shit' sounds about right. Its texture is analogous to the yolk of a soft-boiled egg. My common sense told me that if I touched it then, the firm-looking outer layer would give and my finger would 'dip in shit'. Although that wouldn't go so far as to make me a 'dipshit', the dent in the soft-hearted 'macaroon' would dent my respectability in the eyes of my cousins, who were all older than me and whose respect I was courting. 于是我告诉自己:耐心,耐心,让它干燥几天,然后再来试试。Thereupon, I decided to exercise restraint and patience and give it a few days to dry and set, before I would do anything to it.

接下来的三天,都是风和日丽的大晴天,那滩鸡屎每天沐浴在阳光下,很快变成了深棕色,体积变小了,表皮也完全干燥了,更像杏元饼干。Three mild, sunny days followed. The subject matter of my observation, basking daily in the sun, was quickly tanned to a dark brown. It also became smaller and the skin was completely dry. Now it looked even more like a half macaroon. 我很有把握,这坨(现在不是"滩",而是"坨"了)鸡屎,一定从里到外都是干透了,我没有用树枝试试,就直接用手指摁了摁……I was positive that this wad, no, this lump of dung was dry to the core. I was so sure that I didn't even bother to test it with a twig. I went ahead and poked it with my finger… 嗟,手指陷进去了！Pop! Oops… the 'crust' broke and my finger sank in! 我一下子慌了,看看没人注意,立即把沾了鸡屎的手指在墙上擦了擦,然后到屋后溪流边用一片粗糙的树叶把那根手指狠狠地擦洗了一番。I was overcome more with panic than with disgust. I surveyed my immediate environment. Luckily, nobody was looking this way. I wiped the soiled finger on the wall and walked to the brook behind Gran's house, where I washed that finger after a hard scrub with a rough leaf. 回来时,我注意到,墙上留下了一个不太显眼的、黑乎乎的手指印。When I came back, I saw a dark, inconspicuous fingerprint on the wall.

两年后,我父母带我回崇明看望奶奶。大人在说话,我和堂表姐们就到屋后摘锦灯笼吃。Two years later, my parents took me back to Chongming for a visit. While they were catching up on family news with Gran, my cousins and I went behind the house to pick Chinese lanterns (gooseberries).

绕到屋后的野果园,得经过那面墙。我特意瞟了一眼墙上的那个部位……啊!那个神秘派物理学实验证据,那件壁画杰作,那个不太显眼的、黑乎乎的手指印,还在!We had to walk past that wall on our way to the wild overgrown orchard for some PYO fun. I darted a quick glance at that spot on the wall to see if the evidence of my 'hands-on' research in an esoteric branch of physics was still there... Yes, it was. That *pièce de résistance* of mine - the dark, inconspicuous fingerprint!

英文里不是有个说法,"好奇害死猫"吗?我的好奇心,后果没那么严重,但那个事件的教训,却让我终生受益,从此我再也没有因好奇而"亲手"试验动物粪便的干湿和软硬了。'Curiosity killed the cat.' My curiosity didn't kill me, but it did 'scar' me for life, in the sense that from then on, I never experimented with or 'dabbled' in any animal poo, one way or another, with my own hands.

下放生活结束了,我们离开戴南回城前,就把郭逗和插刀送给了村里的朋友,因为城里无法养鸡。Just before we moved back to Xinghua at the end of my parents' compulsory stint in the countryside, we gave Godot and Swordsman to a friend in the village. The county town was a more 'urban' setting and, as such, was far less fowl-friendly. 跟郭逗、插刀告别的那天,我伤透了心。It was a very sad day for me when I had to say goodbye to them.

小黄出走   Goodbye, Gingerlet

所幸的是，很多年后，我跟另外两个小伙伴——黑狮和小黄——却不存在告别的问题，因为他们俩是自己"出走"的。Many years later, however, saying goodbye to my other two friends, Leonoir and Gingerlet, was surprisingly easy, because there was no farewell to bid: Both had walked out on us.

我们一两天见不着小黄，是很正常的。他不用我们操心，喜欢过自由自在的生活，在野外奔跑、捕猎，只要不下雨，没有淋成落汤猫，他是可以不用回家的。家，对他而言，就是栖身之所，有几个老友，跟他进行一些亲切互动（偶尔还欺负欺负他、抢他嘴里的鱼），还有他爱喝的粥，永不断供。家，是锦上添花。It was quite normal if we didn't see Gingerlet for a day or two. We kept him on a very long leash. He enjoyed his semi-feral lifestyle, footloose and fancy-free. Running around and hunting in the wild was his thing. For Gingerlet, home was a 'shelter from the storm'（so he wouldn't get drenched in a downpour）; home was where he experienced petting and brotherly interactions（such as getting bullied now and again and, occasionally, getting his piscine prey robbed, among other things）; home was where he could have a bowl of delicious congee whenever he fancied it. For a survivor like him, if life could be compared to a cake, then home was the icing on the cake.

有一天我在家正做着作业，父亲从旁边走过。他问："小黄三天唔没回来了，是伐？"我抬头想了想："是呀，怎么回事？"父亲咂了一下嘴，叹了口气，说："伊欢喜瞎跑，格趟可能跑得忒远了，弗认得回来格路了。过两天还是可能自家跑回来格。"One day, I was doing my homework when my father passed by and asked me, 'Gingerlet hasn't been home for three days now, has he?' I looked up, thought about it and said, 'Oh yeah, I wonder what's happened to him.' Father clicked his tongue and sighed, 'He likes to go off the beaten track, but I think he went too far this time and got lost. Maybe he will turn up in a few days' time.'

那个瞬间，我脑海里出现了一幅图景：黎明，旷野，小黄迈着轻盈而自信的步伐，走向天边。At that precise moment, an image popped into my head. It was an image of a vast expanse of wilderness waking up at daybreak. Gingerlet is sauntering, light-pawed and surefooted, towards the horizon.

喵星侠客小黄再也没有回家，我对他的记忆，至今全部浓缩在那幅图景里了。Gingerlet, the dashing knight from Planet Feline, never came home. Whenever I think of him today, I visualise that same picture in my head. It captures, in a nutshell, all that I remember of him.

黑狮迷踪　Adieu, Leonoir

黑狮出走，跟小黄的情况不一样。'Walking out on us' wasn't exactly accurate when describing how Leonoir left us. He did go walkabout too, but he had a different reason. 当时我已经去扬州上高中了，在寄宿学校，寒暑假才回兴化。It happened when I was attending a high school in Yangzhou as a boarder. Yangzhou was about 60 miles from Xinghua. That distance was a big deal in those days. It meant three hours each way on a crowded and uncomfortable coach crawling along a dusty, partially tarmacked highway that was full of potholes and other surprises. That's why I was never home except on summer and winter holidays. 有段时间，父亲经常到乡下"蹲点"，一呆就是半个月到一个月，而母亲组织的群众文艺活动如火如荼，把她忙得焦头烂额，加班加点是家常便饭，经常很晚才能回家。Around that time, my father regularly worked on secondment at fish farms away from the county town, up to four weeks at a stretch. Meanwhile, my mother was snowed under with work, organising community recreational events（music, dance and stuff like that）as part of a nationwide political campaign that was in full swing. Working overtime and getting home very late in the evening was commonplace. 这样一来，黑狮就可能一整天都没东西吃，因为天热，早上不能多给，否则到了中午就馊了，何况他还挑食，不像其他的狗，在外面可以自行解决温饱。父母合计了一下，决定让父亲蹲点时带上黑狮。A net result of that was the potential risk of starvation for Leonoir. They couldn't give him all the food he needed for the rest of the day in one go, because food would go off after just a few hours on a hot day. His partiality for a vegetarian diet also made him an odd man out in his canine community where scavenging was the order of the day. My parents agreed on a solution: Whenever my father went on one of those short stints at a fish farm, he

Leonoir and Gingerlet 伙伴行

would take Leonoir with him.

有一年,我放暑假回到家里,发现黑狮不见了,父母这才惴惴焉把坏消息告诉了我。I found out Leonoir had gone missing when I got home from Yangzhou at the start of one of my summer vacations. My parents gently broke the news to me, self-reproach written all over their faces. 就在上个月,我父亲因工作需要,半途回城,在家里只住一宿,第二天就回到那个渔场,觉得没必要让黑狮来回奔波折腾,所以走之前就把黑狮托付给房东照看一天。Back in June, on one of his trips to the countryside, my father had had to return to Xinghua to pick up something in his office halfway through his stay. He was to spend one night at home and go back to the fish farm the next day. He saw no point in putting Leonoir through the same hassle, so he asked his landlord to look after him, just for a day. 第二天,父亲回到渔场,房东告诉他:"你走了之后,你家的狗不肯吃饭,呜咽了好一阵子,然后就出去了,可能是去找你。村里有人看到西河里有只黑狗游到了对岸。晚上看他没回来,我们出去找,没找到。今天也没回来。唉,对不起了。" The next day, my father went back to the fish farm only to be told by the landlord that Leonoir had gone AWOL. 'Your dog refused to eat after you left. He kept whimpering. Then he went out, looking for you, probably. A villager saw a black dog swimming across the west river. He didn't come back last night, so we did a search in the neighbourhood. We couldn't find him. He hasn't turned up today either. I am very sorry.'

就这样,黑狮离开了我们的生活,永远离开了我的世界。That's how Leonoir left us. That's how Leonoir disappeared from my world. 至今我都不敢去想,他走出那家人的屋子,踏上寻找主人之路,是怀着怎样的一种心情。To this day, it still pains me to speculate what Leonoir had on his mind - and indeed in his heart - as he stepped out of the landlord's house and embarked on his quest to reunite with his loving old friend and caretaker. 渔场,自然是一个水网密布、阡陌纵横的地区,连自行车都极为罕见,当地邮递员得靠小船和自行车相结合的"多式联

- 145 -

运",才能到达各个大队。每当他们骑着车在村里穿行时,后面总是跟着一群看新奇的孩子。The fish farm was, by definition, criss-crossed with waterways of varying sizes and narrow pathways. It had so much water and so little dry land that even bicycles were rare. The postmen had to use an 'intermodal transport system', travelling by boat when on water and by bike when on land. Whenever they were on their two-wheeled vehicle going from door to door through the village, there would be a swarm of kids excitedly chasing after this mechanical rarity. 所以黑狮很快就无法凭气味继续寻觅到回家的路了,也许正因为如此,他虽然不喜欢游泳,但觉得只有勉力游过那条河,才能在对岸重新找到主人的气味。For the same reason, Leonoir would not have gone very far by following the scent. That's probably why he decided to overcome his aversion to swimming and struggle across that river, in a forlorn attempt to pick up my father's trail again on the other side.

  后来,每当想起黑狮凫水渡河的那一幕,我都会问自己:在那个陌生世界里,黑狮是怎样茫然无助,以为被主人抛弃了。黑狮,你去向了何方?In the years that followed, whenever the image of Leonoir swimming across a river flashed into my mind, I would ask myself: What did destiny have in store for Leonoir, lost, hurt, confused and disoriented, in a world of strangers?

Leonoir and Gingerlet 伙伴行

蓦然回首 Was It Real or Was It a Dream?

大约三年过去后，有一天，我在城里突然瞥见一位满脸风霜的农民，身后跟着一条黑狗，那狗乍一看，跟黑狮长得极像。Three years later, give or take, I was walking in town when I saw a dog that was a spitting image of Leonoir. He was trotting behind a farmer who had a weathered and leathered face. By the looks of it, the farmer was the dog's owner. 我立即小心翼翼地跟上，但依然保持一定的距离，从不同的角度观察这只黑狗：小圆眼、卷尾、竖耳，胸口一朵"白领结"！天哪，他不是和黑狮一个模子刻出来的另一只狗，他就是黑衣绅士——黑狮！I closed in, but maintained a safe distance. I pussyfooted round to suss out this Leonoir lookalike from different angles. Small round eyes, check; curled up tail, check; upright ears, check...（take a deep breath for this）*a white tie on his chest, check*! Guess what? He wasn't just a dead ringer for Leonoir. He wasn't Leonoir's alter ego. He was Leonoir, the Dark-Suited Gentleman himself!

我知道，狗的记忆力不亚于大象，这时我只要轻轻发出"哟"的声音，黑狮就会立即回头，扑向我的怀抱！I knew that I was only an "sss" away from a reunion with Leonoir, who undoubtedly had, as dogs do, as much power of memory retention as elephants. He would, on cue, turn round, jump into the air and lunge into my arms! 但我没有这么做。他们俩看上去很有默契，也许这几年一直相依为命，我不忍心拆散他们。But I stopped myself. I couldn't bring myself to end Leonoir's allegiance to his new friend. The rapport between them was palpable. They might only have each other, for all I knew, and I wasn't going to separate them for my own sake.

于是我一言不发，远远地跟着他们，一直跟到城东。我的心吊到了嗓子眼，肚子里翻江倒海，眼眶里噙着的泪，即将夺眶而出，但我狠命地把它压了下去,我知道,我只要发出一点响动,哪怕只是呜咽,就一定会引起黑狮的注意。I carried on shadowing them quietly, again at a safe distance. My heart was in my mouth, my guts were churning, I was feeling the prick of tears, but I fought hard to keep the floodgates firmly shut, lest Leonoir's hypersensitive aural radars should detect my snivelling. I followed them all the way to the east gate of the town. 这条路,当年黑狮在来我家前一定蹒跚着徘徊过多次。This was the path that Leonoir must have tottered along, back and forth, any number of times, before he was adopted by us. 黑狮原本是条流浪小狗。某个暴雨如注的傍晚,母亲的好友万阿姨在下班路上,看到路边人家的屋檐下蜷缩着一只小黑狗,他浑身湿透,在刺骨寒风中瑟瑟发抖,于是动了恻隐之心,把他抱回家了,虽然她家已经有一条名叫小灰的狗,养两只狗超出了她家的经济承受力。He was a foundling, picked up by Auntie Wan, a good friend of my mother's. Wan saw him on her way home from work one day. It was early evening and it was raining cats and dogs. Well, there were no cats in sight, but Wan spotted a pair of soulful, woeful eyes, twinkling behind sheets of water in the torrential downpour. They were the eyes of a black puppy shivering in the perishing cold under the eaves of a street-facing house, drenched. She already had a dog and couldn't afford to keep two. Stung by compassion, however, she made a snap decision and took him home. 次日,万阿姨把小狗带到单位,劝我母亲收留他。她几乎没费什么口舌,母亲就欣然同意了——母亲一想到我看见这团软乎乎的小家伙时欢呼雀跃的模样,就无法拒绝了。从此我家就多了一名成员…… The next day, Wan brought the puppy to work and talked my mother into adopting it. It didn't take much persuasion for my mother to say yes, because she could imagine her son would be over the moon when he saw this adorable ball of fluff. The rest is history.

现在,黑狮和他的朋友,以及像风筝一样,飘在后头的我,走在这条浓缩了黑狮生命史的青石板路上,似乎一起回溯着一个已经完结了的故事——从尾声到序幕。Right now, one man and his dog - and a hanger-on in tow - were walking on this path whose flagstones where inscribed with the life of Leonoir, as if they were retracing a story, from its finale back to its beginning.

出了城门，他们继续前行，我停下脚步，目送黑狮和他的朋友渐渐远去，消失在城外马路的尽头。One man and his dog left the town. The stalker stopped. He watched as Leonoir and his friend walked on. Eventually, they disappeared beyond the far end of the asphalted road.

路的尽头，豁然开阔。那是天边。And the road ended where the vista opened up. Where horizon unfolded.

写在最后　Last But Not Least

　　我和动物伙伴们的故事，就此打住。否则，絮絮叨叨没完没了，读者会腻味。何况即便故事本身意犹未尽，讲故事的人却已意兴阑珊，再勉为其难只会暴殄天物了。Now, have we got to the point where I should wrap up? I think so. Those are the main stories of me and my animal buddies. I don't want to go on forever and spin an interminable yarn of tedium. Worse still, the momentum of the narrative may peter out before the reserve of delicious stories on this topic marshalled from my memory is depleted. 也许我接下来会再写一本书，但写什么，我现在毫无头绪。What I am going to write about in my next book, if there *is* a next book, is still unknown to myself at this point in time. 书也是生命体，内有灵魂支撑，外有命运点拨。倘若某日我们的轨道交集，而我有义务带它进入这个世界的话，它就会"应运而生"，就像这本书。A book is an organism. It has a soul that resides within and a destiny that steers its course. When its path crosses mine and I'm the one to bring it into manifestation, it will be born, willed and encouraged by its own destiny. Like this book.

　　在我的成长岁月里，我有幸从父母那里耳濡目染"无保留的爱"这个真谛。Throughout my formative years, it was what my parents did on a day-to-day basis that showed me what parental affection, a byword for unconditional love, was really about. 在那个年代，在我们那样的普通中国家庭，父母不习惯把"我爱你"之类的字眼挂在嘴边，但我的寸草之心，却能真切感受到他们无言的舐犊春晖，在无微不至地沐浴着我。孩提时代的我，不知道诸如"无常"这样的哲理，五味杂陈的大千世界于我而言，多半是未知数，是无法把握的，唯有这种亲情，能带来恒久不变的踏实。In those days, in an average Chinese family like mine, it was uncommon for parents to articulate 'I love you' in these explicit

Leonoir and Gingerlet 伙伴行

words to their children, but throughout my childhood, I could sense breezes of love in its purest form enveloping me in lulling silence. It was unfathomable but tangible. It was part of the air I breathed. It was the only certainty in a world of bittersweet vagaries that were largely elusive to me as a child, who had yet to grasp such philosophical abstractions as impermanences and transiencies.

除了父母的养育和言传身教之恩外,那些动物伙伴们的一路陪伴,也是我成长故事中的一条平行线。I am indebted to my parents for bringing me into this experience-rich world, for bringing me up with sacrifice and dedication and for bringing me to my senses as I toddled along in the early part of my life. In parallel to this trajectory of my early life was my association with the animal friends featured in this book. 跟他们交流的主要媒介是眼神,这是一种超越语言、无法概念化的"神交",神交的主旋律,是陪伴与温情。Communication with them was primarily through the eyes. It was a silent 'communion', devoid of human memes. The theme of such exchange was heart-warming, affectionate companionship. 不同的人,也许有不同的体验,但我并非出于情感需要臆测"鱼之乐",那种真实的感受至今依然鲜活如初。Make of that what you will, but this conviction of mine, which is very much alive even to this day, did not stem from an imagined vicarious experience that merely served to supply an emotional need in me. 那一个个灵魂,相继来到我的世界,走一遭,途中因缘际会与我相遇,命运的轨迹并行一段,我们相伴相依若干年。All those individual souls came to the world I was born into, to spend a lifetime here. On the way, a concatenation of serendipitous circumstances brought us together. The river of their destiny and that of mine merged and flowed as one for some years, during which we kept each other company. 然后,各自的命运又把我们拆散,欢乐时光,句点总是无奈的告别,但既是相互独立的灵魂,必有自己的路要走,走不同的路。Then, at some point, our respective destinies decided to move *on*, but *apart*. So we did. The happy time we spent together was invariably punctuated with a full stop of farewell. That could not be helped: At the end of the day, our souls are independent of each other. Each has its own path to follow and no path is the same as the next one. 茫然中，有种了然；了然，便释然，还有欣然。There is a 'found' in the 'lost': Through the lost past, an understanding is found. Through the new-found understanding, the baggage of the past is lost and the beauty of the past is re-found and internalised. 继续前行时，我已不是从前的我。但往昔的云彩，并未消散于回眸间，当年的清泉，走过四季，已化作醇浆，化作妙音，在舌尖滑过，安抚甜酸苦辣的溃涝，将悲欢离合的滞重，抛向如歌的云端。As life matches on, I am no longer the me of old. But the snows of yesteryear have not vanished in the heat of *now*. They have taken on a patina of autumnal hues and brewed into something mellow and, ultimately, mellifluent, to be savoured by the tastebuds that have survived the ravages of life's pungency and the assaults of life's poignancy. 一段段点亮虚空的善缘，带着生命的轻重，温暖并丰富了我的人生内涵，我的路向前延伸，延伸到我看不见的地方，我一路体验的种种美好，必将在我内心深处永驻，伴我深一脚浅一脚，走向天边。就像小黄。就像黑狮。The connections I have had with other kindly souls, each a microcosm of life lived and life experienced, have been enriching my own life and keep-

远方的地平线。*Horizons yonder*.

ing it warm. My path stretches ahead, beyond the range of my vision. All the goodness I have been blessed with will forever reside in my heart of hearts, as I soldier on in my peregrination towards the horizon, with or without fair winds and following seas. The way Gingerlet did. The way Leonoir did.

Geneva, Switzerland
7th July 2015

图书在版编目（CIP）数据

伙伴行 / 季晨著述. -- 南京：南京大学出版社，2017.4
ISBN 978-7-305-18408-6

Ⅰ.①伙… Ⅱ.①季… Ⅲ.①中国文学－当代文学－作品综合集－汉、英 Ⅳ.①I217.2

中国版本图书馆CIP数据核字（2017）第062233号

出版发行	南京大学出版社
社　　址	南京市汉口路22号　邮编　210093
出 版 人	金鑫荣

书　　名	伙伴行
著　　述	季　晨
责任编辑	胡　豪　　编辑热线　025-83594071
照　　排	南京紫藤制版印务中心
印　　刷	南京玉河印刷厂
开　　本	889×1194　1/24　印张　6.6　字数　150千
版　　次	2017年4月第1版　2017年4月第1次印刷
ISBN	978-7-305-18408-6
定　　价	29.50元

网　　址	http://www.NjupCo.com
新浪微博	http://e.weibo.com/njuyzxz
官方微信号	njupress
销售咨询热线	025-83594756

* 版权所有，侵权必究
* 凡购买南大版图书，如有印装质量问题，请与所购
  图书销售部门联系调换